THE WORLD OF SCIENCE
SEAS AND OCEANS

THE WORLD OF SCIENCE
SEAS AND OCEANS

DAVID LAMBERT & ANITA McCONNELL

Facts On File Publications
New York, New York ● Bicester, England

SEAS AND OCEANS

Copyright © Macdonald & Co (Publishers) Ltd
1985, 1987

First published in the United States of America in
1985 by Facts on File, Inc., 460 Park Avenue South,
New York, N.Y.10016

First published in Great Britain in 1985 by Orbis
Publishing Limited, London

**Library of Congress Cataloging in Publication
Data**

Main entry under title:

World of Science

Includes index.
Summary: A twenty-five volume encyclopedia of
scientific subjects, designed for eight- to twelve-year-
olds. One volume is entirely devoted to projects.
1. Science—Dictionaries, Juvenile.   1. Science—
Dictionaries
Q121.J86   1984   500   84-1654

ISBN: 0-8160-1064-1

Printed in Yugoslavia
10 9 8 7 6 5 4 3 2

Consultant editors
Eleanor Felder, former managing editor, *Scientific
American*
James Neujahr, Dean of the School of Education, City
College of New York
Ethan Signer, Professor of Biology, Massachusetts
Institute of Technology
J. Tuzo Wilson, Director General, Ontario Science
Centre

Previous pages A
huge brain coral
growing on the
seaward side of a reef
in the tropics.

Editor Penny Clarke
Designer Roger Kohn

CONTENTS

Note There are some unusual words in this book. They are explained in the Glossary on page 62. The first time each word is used in the text it is printed in *italics*.

◀ The great jaws of a sperm whale break the the ocean's surface. It belongs to the group of whales known as the toothed whales, although it only has teeth on its lower jaw. Each tooth is 20cm (8in) long.

OUR WATERY WORLD

North Pole

80   Arctic Ocean

70

Arctic Circle

60

50   North America

Rocky Mountains

40

30

Tropic of Cancer

20

Pacific Ocean

10

180 170 140 130 120 110 100 90 80 70 60 50 40 30 20 10
Equator

10

Andes   South America

20   Tropic of Capricorn

Atlantic   Ocean

30

40   Atlantic   Ocean

50

60

Antarctic Circle   Antarctic Circle

70

80   Antarctic   Antarctic

South Pole   South Pole

5000
3000
2000
500
200 +
0   0
- 200
2000
4000
6000
8000

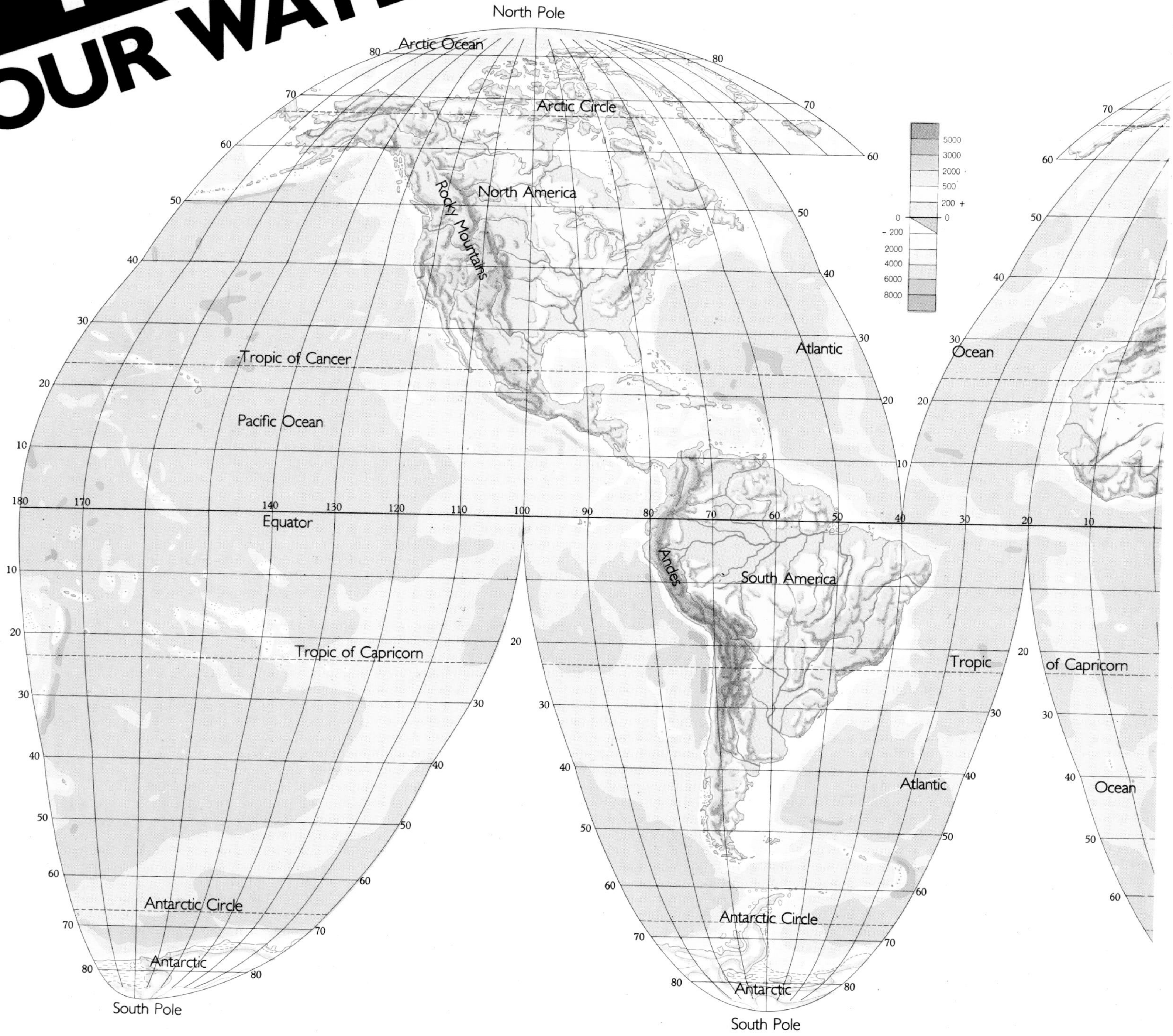

THE OCEANS

Oceans are basins in the Earth's surface containing salt water. At present they cover about seven-tenths of the globe. In atlases you will see four great areas of water, these are the oceans. They are partly separated by vast continental land masses. The smaller areas, called seas, contain water that is rather different from the oceans; it may be fresher or saltier; warmer or colder. Throughout the Earth's history water has been added to the oceans from the volcanoes that erupt both under water and on land. But it does not remain in the seas and oceans. It is constantly *evaporating* and forming clouds and rain. Then the rain, where it has

▼ This map shows the
huge area of the
Earth's surface covered
by the oceans. The
Arctic Ocean, around
the North Pole, is the
coldest of all. The
Atlantic and Pacific
oceans stretch from the
far north to the far
south. The southern
ends of these two and
that of the Indian
Ocean surround the
coldest continent,
Antarctica.

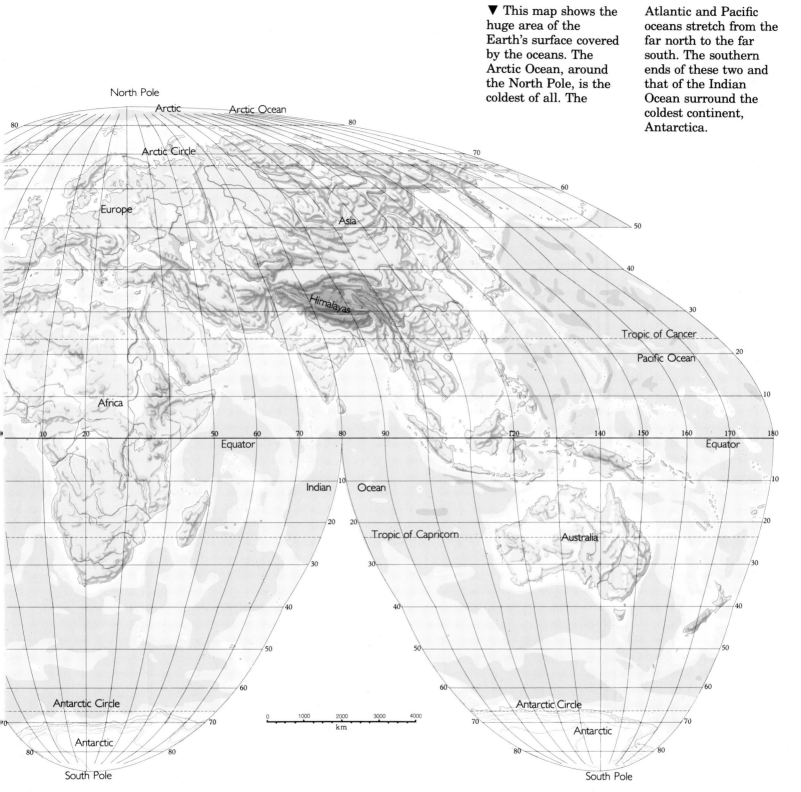

fallen on the land runs back into streams and rivers and so into the seas and oceans once more. As the continents have grown and been worn away, as the polar ice has melted and then frozen again, so the level of water in the oceans has risen and then fallen to cover more or less of the Earth's surface.

The four oceans
If you could divide the Earth's water into 100 parts, 97 would lie in the seas and oceans. The Pacific Ocean is by far the largest ocean. This vast stretch of water lies west of the Americas and east of Australia and Asia. The Pacific covers almost as much of the Earth's surface as

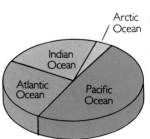

▲ The relative sizes of the Earth's main oceans.

7

the other oceans put together. All continents would fit inside it. The Pacific is also the deepest ocean, with an average depth of 4280m (14,050ft). In fact part of the Mindanao Trench – the deepest part in any ocean – lies 11.5km (7.1 miles) below sea level. That depth would drown Mount Everest which, at 8806m (29,038ft) is the highest mountain peak on land.

The Atlantic is the second largest ocean. It covers just under half the area of the Pacific and is not as deep – the average depth is 3330m (10,930ft). The Atlantic separates Europe and Africa from the Americas.

The Indian Ocean is rather smaller than the Atlantic, but its average depth is slightly greater. Its margins are Asia, Australia and Africa.

The Arctic Ocean lies north of North America and Asia and is the smallest and shallowest ocean. Its average depth is only 990m (3250ft).

The salty oceans

Various salts and minerals give sea water its bitter taste. Three-quarters of the salt is the same as we use in our food. If you dried out 1kg (2.2lb) of sea water, you would be left with about 35g (1¼oz) of salt, whichever ocean you had taken it from, although the salt content of smaller areas of sea water, for example, fiords and estuaries, varies. When sea water evaporates, most of the salt is left behind and rain and rivers continually wash in more from soil and rocks. But the oceans do not get more and more salty because salt is trapped with the mud and sand that builds up on the sea floor. In this way the *salinity* of the oceans has stayed constant for millions of years.

The temperature of sea water

There is great variation in water temperature throughout the earth's seas and oceans. In summer, the temperature of the water at the surface of the Red Sea between Africa and Arabia can rise to 30°C (86°F). In the open ocean, near the equator, it can reach 28°C (82°F). By contrast, in the Arctic winters sea temperatures fall to −2°C (28°F) – the temperature at which sea water freezes.

The Sun's heat cannot penetrate below about 200m (660ft) and at this depth there are no waves to stir the waters up to the surface to be warmed. In fact, most ocean water lies even deeper with a chilly average temperature of 3.8°C (39°F).

Crushing pressure

At sea level the atmosphere presses with a force of 1 kilo on each square centimetre of your body (14.7 pounds per square inch). As you go down into the sea, the pressure increases rapidly. In the greatest ocean depths it is a thousand times greater than at the surface, reaching one tonne per square centimetre (3.1 tons per square inch) – pressure that could crush any ordinary submarine.

So most of the seas and oceans are pitch dark, cold and under great pressure. Nevertheless, life has adapted to these hostile conditions and marine organisms are found at every level, both in the water and on the sea floor.

The shades of the sea

A glass of water is transparent, yet the sea looks blue or greenish brown when we see it from the deck of a boat or from the air. This is partly due to the way that sunlight is scattered through it and absorbed at different depths. Sunlight is made up of a 'spectrum' of hues from red, through orange, yellow and green, to blue. It is the blue end of this spectrum that penetrates furthest into the water, so in clear seas divers find that everything becomes more blue as they descend.

Near the coast, water takes on a green, yellow or brown tinge. This is due to the vast numbers of microscopic plants floating near the surface and also to the mud that rivers discharge into the sea. These areas, however, contain many plants, fish and other forms of animal life, whereas the clear blue tropical oceans are 'deserts', with little life.

▼ These heaps of sea salt were gathered from the Mediterranean Sea at Trapani, Sicily. First sea water in shallow pools is allowed to evaporate. Then the crust of salt left behind by the evaporating water is raked into heaps to drain before the salt is finally dried.

WAVES AND TIDES

▼ Strong winds seize a wave crest and hurl it forward. The long streaks of windblown spray are known as spindrift. The photograph gives some idea of the immense force let loose by a breaking ocean wave.

spring tides

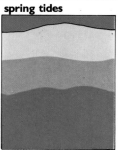

neap tides

| ☐ sea | ☐ beach |
| ☐ tidal range | ☐ land |

Most of us have seen the wind stir the sea's surface. We have noticed, too, that the level of the sea falls and rises with the tides. Both these changes involve waves.

Wind-driven waves

Wind stirs the ocean surface into waves that we can see moving through the water. Waves are parallel rows of watery ridges, with valleys between. Each ridge is a wave crest, and each valley is a trough. The distance from one wave crest to the next is called the wave length. The height from the bottom of one trough to the top of the next crest is the wave's height.

Wave lengths and heights depend partly on the wind that pushes waves along. High winds, blowing for long periods across wide expanses of water, raise the longest, highest waves. Out in the open ocean, strong winds can build rounded waves called swells with a wave length of about 1km ($\frac{1}{2}$ mile). Storm waves that rear up as they near a shore may tower to a height of 34m (112ft).

Each wave seems to move a mass of water along. But if we watch a floating log just bobbing up and down as a wave passes, we realize, that this is not so. In fact, as a wave crest passes, it lifts water particles, moves them forward, then drops them. Each particle travels up, forward, down and back, so it simply goes around in a circle.

But something different happens when a wave sweeps in to a shelving shore. In water less than half a wavelength deep, water particles at the bottom of the circle catch on the sea floor. This slows down the bottom of the wave. The upper part races on, growing steeper, until its crest spills forward and it surges foaming up the shore.

Tsunamis

Storm waves can travel at 55km (34 miles) an hour, but the fastest waves are those set off by underwater earthquakes or volcanoes. These waves are called by their Japanese name: tsunamis. A tsunami can cross the Pacific Ocean at up to 800km (500 miles) an hour. At sea the wave may be too low for ships' passengers to notice. But tsunamis entering a shallow bay may rear 67m (220ft). Such waves swamp low coasts, sometimes drowning thousands of people.

How tides work

Twice a day, on most coasts, the tide creeps up the beach and then retreats. Some places have four tides a day; others have a rise and fall that is too small to be noticed.

The main cause of the tides is the Moon's pull upon the earth. As it circles round the globe, the moon pulls upon the oceans facing it. So the waters rise in a bulge towards the moon. On the opposite side of the earth, where the moon's pull is weakest, there is another bulge. If there were no continents in the way these bulges would travel round the world following the moon. In fact, we do not see this simple pattern. The Sun also attracts the ocean waters, though less strongly, and the shape of the sea bed, and the surrounding coasts, all help to delay or speed up these great travelling waves or bulges. Each part of each ocean has its own revolving tide wave and high tides sweep up one side of the ocean and down the other – clockwise in the northern hemisphere and anticlockwise (counter clockwise) south of the equator. There are tides in the enclosed seas, such as the Baltic and Mediterranean, but the range of the rise and fall of water is much less, often only a few centimetres (inches).

▶ Spring tides occur when the Sun and Moon line up and pull upon the sea together. Neap tides occur when Sun and Moon pull at right angles, and each pull tends to cancel out the other. Each kind of tide happens about twice a month. Spring tides have the highest rise and the lowest fall. They occur near new moon and full moon. Neap tides have the smallest range. They occur when the Moon is in its first and last quarters.

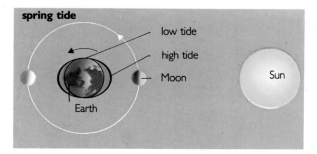

spring tide — low tide — high tide — Moon — Sun — Earth

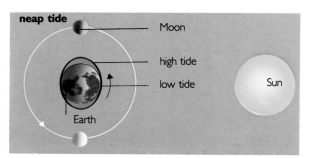

neap tide — Moon — high tide — low tide — Sun — Earth

◀ The Severn Bore is a wall of water that surges many miles up England's River Severn. A river bore is a wave caused when a rising tide meets the water flowing down the river. The Severn Bore can reach a height of 1.5m (5ft).

▼ Limp seaweed and pools of sea water show a seashore at low tide. At high tide the sea will swirl in and drown this stretch of shore.

OCEAN CURRENTS

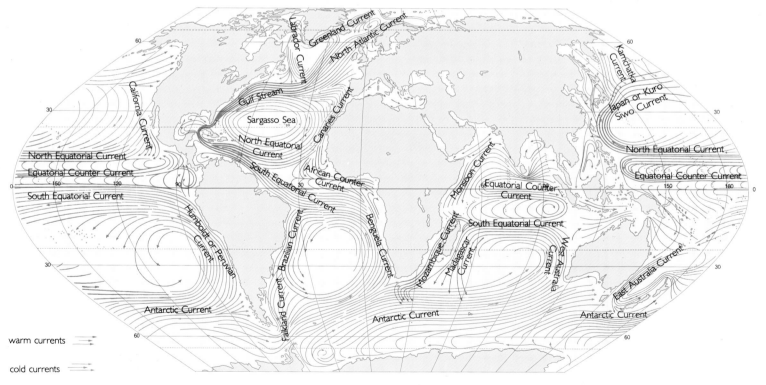

warm currents

cold currents

▲ Surface currents tend to flow clockwise around oceans in the northern half of the world, anticlockwise in the south. Warm water from the tropics moves toward chilly polar regions. Cold water from polar regions moves toward the tropics. This flow helps to spread heat around the world.

Underwater currents have a rather different pattern of circulation from currents flowing at the surface. Many flow in the opposite direction to the currents on the surface. Deep-sea drift carries cold, dense water many thousands of miles from its starting places in the polar oceans.

11

People have called ocean currents 'rivers in the sea'. But most are far broader and deeper than any river flowing over land, and indeed the whole vast body of ocean water is in constant motion.

Surface currents

Winds keep powerful currents moving through the surface waters of all oceans. Near the polar regions, westerly winds try to push water to the east. In the tropics, trade winds tend to push water to the west.

But other factors also affect how currents flow. For instance, the Earth's spin steers currents to the right north of the equator, and to the left south of the equator. Scientists call this the *Coriolis effect* after Gaspard de Coriolis, the French mathematician who discovered it in 1835. Continents that block a current's path also influence its flow, for they force the current to turn aside and change direction sharply.

Gyres

Winds, the Earth's spin and land barriers keep currents flowing around the oceans in giant loops called *gyres*. In the northern hemisphere the water in a gyre flows clockwise. But in the southern hemisphere it travels anticlockwise. Each gyre consists of several currents. Some are warm, some cold.

Take, for instance, the currents of the North Atlantic gyre. In the North Atlantic, the north-east trade winds help to push the warm north equatorial current westward towards the West Indies and the Gulf of Mexico. From here, the narrow Gulf Stream heads north past the south-eastern United States. The Gulf Stream is the fast-flowing edge of the warm Sargasso Sea 700–800m (2300–2600ft) deep. The current meanders to and fro like a mighty river. In places the stream runs at 9km (5½ miles) per hour – the fastest current in the oceans. Off the north-eastern United States south-west winds nudge the Gulf Stream north-eastward. It slows down and splits up into several, weaker, branches. One branch, the North Atlantic Current, brings warm water to the British Isles and Norway. Another branch, the Canaries Current, heads south past the Canary Islands off north-west Africa. Water rising from deep down makes the Canaries Current cold. This current joins the North Equatorial Current, the one we started with.

Other currents contribute to the North Atlantic gyre. Among the most important is the Labrador Current which brings chilly Arctic Ocean water south past eastern Canada. Similar current systems flow around the North Pacific.

Currents of the deep

Ocean currents help to spread heat more evenly around the Earth than would be possible if ocean water just lay still. But not all flow through surface waters. There are also deep-sea currents or '*drifts*'. Their flow helps spread heat through oceans from top to bottom. First, cold, heavy polar water sinks. Then it creeps along the sea floor towards the equator. Next, some of this deep, cold water wells up to replace surface water being blown offshore by steady winds.

In this way, cold, upwelling water feeds chilly currents flowing north off tropical western South America and off south-west Africa. As these currents travel through the tropics the sun gradually warms them.

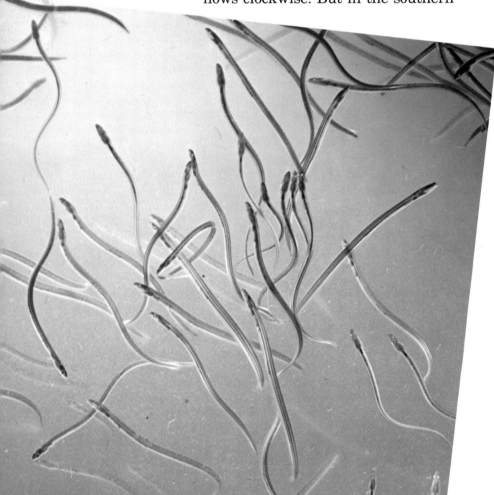

▼ Elvers (baby eels) drift to North America and Europe with the Gulf Stream and North Atlantic current. In this way some eels can migrate farther than any other fish. Their starting point is the Sargasso Sea, a calm area of water inside the North Atlantic gyre.

Sheets, slabs and chunks of ice cover roughly one-tenth of the Earth's oceans. In the far north ice smothers much of the Arctic Ocean. In the far south, ice rims the great island continent of Antarctica. Each summer some ice melts, so the area of frozen sea shrinks. But each autumn, as the temperature drops, ice once more spreads far out across cold polar areas of ocean.

Sea ice
Cold water is heavier than warm water and sinks, so you might expect ice to form on the ocean bed, not on its surface. But when water freezes it expands, and the salt is left behind. Bulk for bulk, then, ice is lighter than water. So ice floats on the sea.

Shallow coastal waters quickly chill through from top to bottom, so these freeze first when the temperature falls. Deeper waters offshore take longer to cool enough to freeze. At first, only a thin film of ice – known as *frazil* ice – covers the sea. Water movement shapes this into thicker slabs. Sailors call these pancake ice. As the cold grows more intense, these ice slabs or *floes* clump and thicken. Then winds and currents jam them together. In places the edge of one flow rides over another to build a tall ridge. Floes packed together like this may form a field of *pack ice* hundreds of miles across. But here and

▲ A sturdy icebreaker easily butts aside thin ice floes in these cold waters off the coast of Canada.

13

► High, narrow icebergs, with tops like castle towers are castellated bergs. Although the sea around is salty, the frozen water in a berg is fresh. People have suggested towing icebergs half way across the world, to bring fresh water to hot, dry lands like southern California and Saudi Arabia, but the icebergs could only be towed slowly, so warm winds and rain would melt them long before they reached the tropics.

▼ A nuclear submarine surfaces amid ice somewhere in the middle of the Arctic Ocean. In 1958 the *USS Nautilus* became the first vessel to cross the Arctic Ocean by sailing underneath its everlasting roof of pack ice.

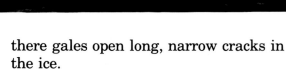

there gales open long, narrow cracks in the ice.

Summer warmth, currents and winds help to break floes off the outer rim of the pack ice. Floes drifting north from the Antarctic pack ice sometimes spread across one-sixth of the Earth's oceans. In the Arctic Ocean, the floes are mostly hemmed in by Asia and North America. But some escape into the Atlantic and Pacific oceans. Those floes that drift into warm waters gradually melt and disappear.

Icebergs
Icebergs are masses of ice that were once part of *glaciers* or ice sheets on land and have now slid or dropped into the sea. Where a glacier – a river of ice – meets the sea, tall bergs may snap off from the

glacier snout. More than 14,000 a year probably enter the sea from the island of Greenland alone. Many are fantastic shapes. Some are 450m (1500ft) thick, but four-fifths of this thickness lies hidden below sea level.

In places the great ice sheet that covers Antarctica reaches the sea as thick, wide ice shelves that jut out into the sea. Slabs that break off look like giant table tops. Some are so thick that their tops are 50m (160ft) above water level. Such floating, flat-topped slabs are called tabular bergs.

Some tabular bergs are immense. At least one has been recorded that was bigger than Belgium, and Belgium has an area of 31,000 sq km (11,775 sq miles)! A monster like that could drift almost to the tropics before it melts completely.

Coping with ice at sea

Icebergs and pack ice make sea travel difficult and dangerous in some ocean areas. Once no ship could pierce the ice that blocked the Arctic Ocean. Now icebreakers plough through all but the thickest pack ice. And nuclear submarines can cruise below it. One day, submarine merchant ships might take a short cut across the Arctic from Atlantic to Pacific ports just as airplanes now fly over it on those same routes.

Icebergs will always be a threat to ships in cold North Atlantic waters. In 1912 the *Titantic*, a great new ocean liner, collided with an unseen iceberg and sank. Now, however, the International Ice Patrol warns of bergs likely to drift south into busy shipping lanes.

▼This map shows the different kinds of sediment that coat the ocean floor. Terrigenous deposits are gravels, sand and silt washed off land. Calcareous ooze contains chalky shells of tiny plankton organisms. Red clay is the finest mud brought down by rivers, with some dust from volcanoes and fallen meteors. Radiolarian ooze and diatom ooze contain the glassy skeletons of tiny organisms from the plankton.

THE OCEAN FLOOR

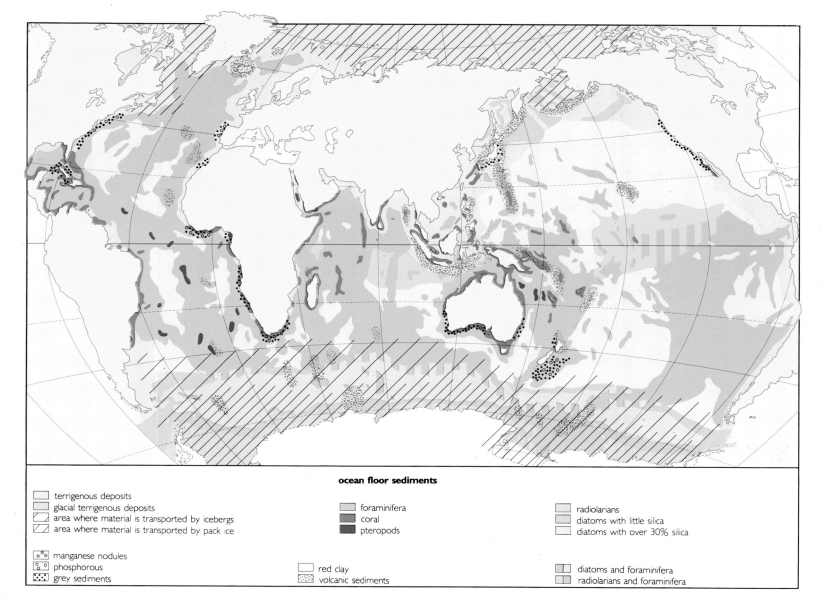

ocean floor sediments

- terrigenous deposits
- glacial terrigenous deposits
- area where material is transported by icebergs
- area where material is transported by pack ice

- manganese nodules
- phosphorous
- grey sediments

- foraminifera
- coral
- pteropods

- red clay
- volcanic sediments

- radiolarians
- diatoms with little silica
- diatoms with over 30% silica

- diatoms and foraminifera
- radiolarians and foraminifera

A voyage across an ocean floor would bring surprises. You would find that, like the land, the ocean has its mountains, plains and valleys.

The continental shelf

Imagine setting off from North America or Europe across the floor of the Atlantic Ocean. At first your route would lie over the gently sloping *continental shelf.* Continental shelves are great rock platforms that surround the continents. Most are about 180m (600ft) below sea level. Some are narrow. Others stretch up to 1200km (750 miles) from the shore. The greater part of these continental shelves stood above the sea long ago when ocean levels were lower. From a deep-sea submarine you would see where rivers had flowed across these lands, now long since drowned. You would also see where currents, waves, and modern river mouths have dumped heaps of gravel, sand and mud. Indeed, loose debris from the land covers most of a continental shelf.

The deep ocean floor

As you move farther out from the shore, the shelf slopes very gently downward. Suddenly, you reach a drop – the steep continental slope. This plunges to the deep ocean floor – 3800m (12,000ft or so) below the ocean surface. Although the ocean floor is solid rock, much of it is covered in a coat of soft ooze. This consists of billions of shells of tiny plants and animals that lived in surface waters, then died and sank.

The deep floor of the open ocean, the *abyss,* is generally flat, although part of the Pacific floor is scarred by vast trenches. Elsewhere rise underwater peaks with flattened tops. There is, too, a mighty chain of underwater mountains, the Mid Ocean Ridge, that runs from north to south down the centre of the Atlantic Ocean, then extends eastwards to the Indian and Pacific oceans.

The spreading ocean floor

Long after they discovered these strange ocean landscapes, scientists puzzled about how the oceans could have been formed, because in the deep sea there is no rain or frost or wind to carve valleys as there is on land.

Now, scientists believe that underwater peaks and trenches are clues to how the ocean floor took shape. They believe that oceanic ridges show where new ocean floor is being made. Molten rock rises from beneath the ocean floor, welling up through a split in the crest of the ridge. The split keeps growing wider, but new rock makes up for this by sticking to the sides of the crack. Far from the ridges, deep trenches form where old ocean floor is being dragged down into the molten depths below the sea bed's solid surface. So although sea bed is being made in one part of an ocean, it is being lost elsewhere.

This helps to explain the flat-topped underwater mountains near some trenches. Peaks once above the sea sink as they near a trench. But waves level off the mountain tops before these slip below the surface.

Scientists reckon that in time all ocean floor gets dragged down into the *mantle* – the layer of hot rock below the earth's solid surface – because scarcely any ocean floor is older than 200 million years.

▼ The flounder, like all flatfish, swims with an undulating movement. Its coloration provides an excellent camouflage as it lies on the sands and gravels on the bottom.

► This community of crabs, fish and molluscs lives where the deep ocean floor splits and material from the Earth's core wells out.

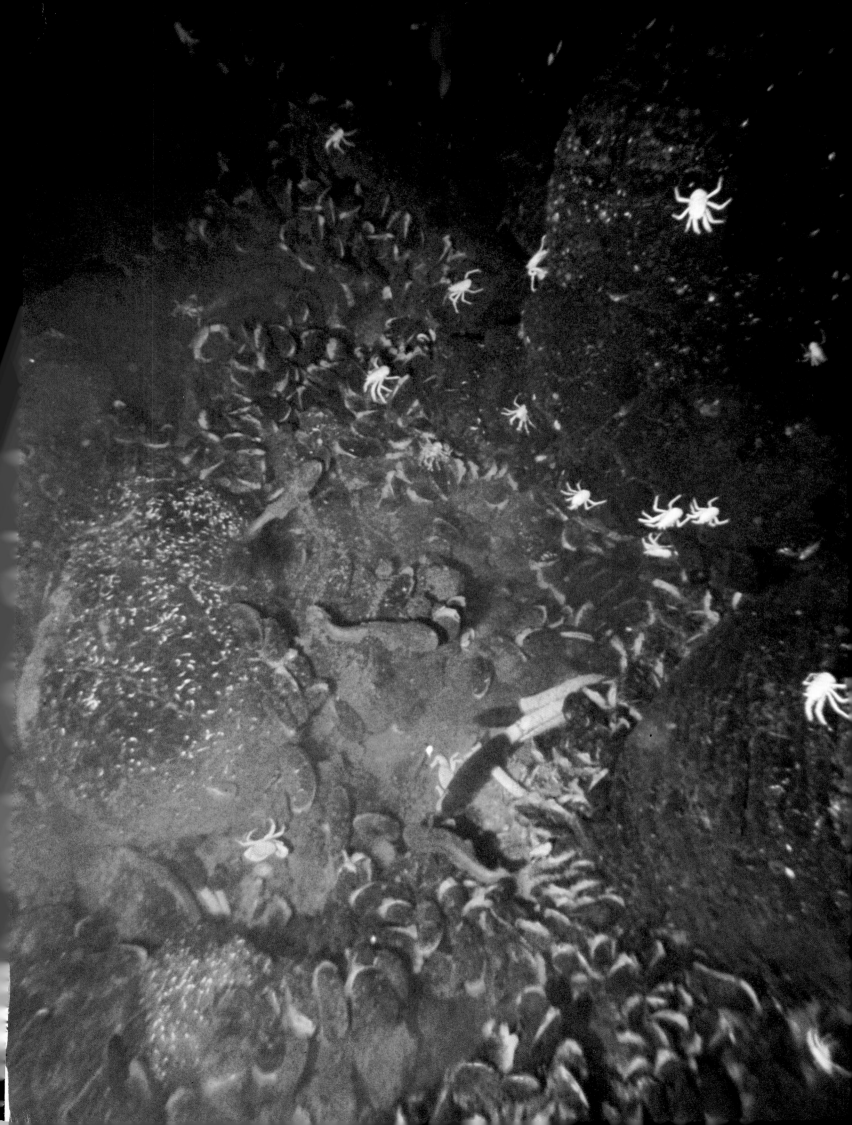

2 SHORES AND ISLANDS

ROCKY COASTS

On a fine, still day a sea cliff is a tranquil place. But when a gale whips up the surface of the sea, few places seem more savage. Then you glimpse a battle in the war between the sea and the land – a war that sea cliffs almost everywhere are losing.

▶ Wave action has cut off this rocky island from the shore, except for a low, wave-washed strip of sand. Such isolated cliffs are called stacks.

▼ Rocky pillars show where the sea is wearing away chunks of cliff. First, waves cut two caves through a narrow headland jutting into the sea. One cave roof has fallen in. Next, the other will collapse. That will leave two rock pillars. In time the waves will level these as well.

The sea's attack
The sea attacks with several weapons. First comes water. Winter storms strike Europe's North Atlantic coasts with waves that pound like hammers. Some crash against the cliffs with a force of 30,000 kilos per square metre (6150 pounds per square foot). This blow rams air into crannies in the sea cliffs. As the waves fall back the air expands with sudden force. Bit by bit this opens up the cracks and loosens chunks of rocks between then. In time these chunks will topple into the sea.

Broken pieces of cliff then become the sea's main weapons of attack. For churning waves smash broken rocks against the cliff and one another. That breaks boulders into stones. It smooths stones into rounded pebbles, and grinds pebbles into grains of sand. Boulders,

stones, pebbles and sand grains dashed against the bottom of a cliff all help to gnaw away its rock.

Meanwhile rain and frost weaken the overhanging cliff above. In time this top heavy mass tumbles down as well.

The sea attacks some limestone cliffs even in calm weather: salt water just dissolves the rock away.

At low tide you can often glimpse the land the sea has won. For where the cliff face used to stand, only a drowned, wave-cut rock platform juts out beyond the shore.

Types of cliff

How the sea gnaws cliffs away depends largely on the rocks of which cliffs are made. Hard rocks like granite resist battering better than softer rocks like clay or chalk. But even hard rock has weaknesses that the sea can widen.

Hard rock tends to wear away slowly, and often forms steep cliffs. But when the sea attacks soft or loose rocks like clay, gravel or sand, these slip downhill. Here, cliffs slope gently toward the sea.

But the steepness of a cliff depends partly on the angle of rock layers in the cliff. Layers that tilt toward the land might give a sloping cliff face. Layers that tilt toward the sea lose chunks of rock in ways that yield a steeper cliff.

Soft and hard rocks reach the sea at different places on many a coast. Often, the hard, resistant rocks jut out into the sea as long peninsulas. Between them, the sea gnaws away soft rock and so cuts deep bays into the land.

HOW BEACHES GROW

Although the sea can wear away the land, it can also help make land, too. For here and there the sea builds beaches from the smashed remains of rocks that waves have broken from a rocky shore. Below sea cliffs of old hard rock that face the open ocean you might find boulder beaches. Here lie massive blocks of rock – some the size of houses – all broken from the cliffs above. Smaller rocks pile up where waves have cut small, partly sheltered coves into the cliff's face.

barnacle   blenny   common tern   prawn   squid   brown seaweed sea anemone   limpet

sea anemone
golden star sea squirts   common shore crab   brittle star   hermit crab with sea anemone on its shell   dog whelk
starfish   solitary sea squirt

Longshore drift

Most beaches are huge, low heaps of loose materials – particularly grains of sand or pebbles. These materials have often travelled many miles along the coast. The main forces that shifted them so far were probably waves breaking at an angle on the shore. Each wave throws sand or gravel up a beach and a little way along it. But the wave's backwash sucks the sand or pebbles straight down towards the sea. This happens time after time. So sand or pebbles can zig-zag far along a coast. Geographers call this kind of journey *longshore drift*.

Meanwhile tidal currents might be shifting masses more loose material along the sea bed just offshore.

Sandy or pebbly beaches grow where they do for several reasons. They form where wind and waves pile sand or pebbles on a gently sloping shore. Beaches also grow where headlands, or those man-made walls called *groynes*, block longshore drift. A small, curved strip of beach might nestle in a rocky cove sheltered by cliff-lined headlands that jut out from each end. In other places

▲ Most of these seashore animals and plants are adapted to life on a rocky shore. Some cling to rocks. Fishes like the blenny hide in rock crevices. Squids swim freely offshore. At low tide you find limpets, sea anemones, crabs and starfish in rock pools.

▲ On this stretch of coast near Naples in Florida, the sea is pushing sand ashore and huge dunes are forming. In the background of the photograph you can see the height that some dunes have already reached.

currents and longshore drifting build long, low beaches known as *bars*, which lie offshore. A beach that grows from a headland out into the sea is called a *spit*.

Pebble beaches

The ingredients of pebble beaches are rounded stones. The smallest stones are no bigger than a fingernail, the largest may be 20cm (8in). These large pebbles are thrown up the shore by storm waves, and the backwash tends to be too weak to drag them back down the beach.

In calm weather, waves add more pebbles than they take away. But when storms rage, the sea can tear away great chunks of pebble beach.

Sandy shores

The beaches most of us know best are made of billions of tiny grains of quartz, often of a golden hue. Some beaches are famous for their coloured sands; black, white, pink or brown sands are quite common in some parts of the world. Once these were ingredients in granite, sandstone or other quartz-rich rocks.

Some sands, though, are the ground-down remains of seashells or coral rock produced by animals or plants.

Sandy beaches tend to slope up from the sea less steeply than pebble beaches. Off some low shores, the *ebbing* tide reveals vast stretches of gently sloping sands that reach for miles into the sea. These sands sometimes rest upon a hidden wave-cut platform of solid rock.

When winds blow up a gently sloping sandy beach they pick up clouds of loose dry sand particles. The wind carries some of this inland. But if it meets obstacles, such as plants, the sand piles up against them. In time this builds sandy hillocks known as *dunes*. Dunes as high as small skyscrapers line low sandy shores in parts of France and Spain.

▶ Billions of particles of coral went to build this sandy beach on the Hawaiian island of Kauai. The coral sands are the remains of coral rock smashed up by waves.

MUDDY SHORES

► Four rivers drain into Morecambe Bay on the north-west coast of England. Here one of them flows across the sands at low tide. The shallow water of the Bay make it a very important habitat for waders and other shore birds.

You can see the grains that make up sand, but most particles in mud are microscopically small. Some are very finely ground-up rock. Others are tiny scraps of dead plant or animal material. Rainwater washes huge amounts of mud off the land and into rivers. There, tiny particles drift downstream toward the sea. So light are these tiny particles that even a gently flowing river current keeps them on the move. Mud sinks and settles only in the calmest fresh water. But where tides bring sea water into an estuary, or where rivers flow into the sea, salt water causes the mud particles to clump together and so they fall to the sea bed as the river current slackens.

Calm waters
In places sand and pebble spits and bars shelter a river's mouth from rough sea waves. Elsewhere mud might settle in protected bays or the wide, low river mouths called *estuaries*. In these calm waters, tiny particles of *silt* and even smaller particles of clay slowly build up muddy carpets just offshore.

Mud carpets can thicken quickly on the floor of a *lagoon* – a shallow stretch of sea almost cut off from the rest, for example by a spit or bar. Each high tide brings more silt particles from the open sea.

Each low tide lets some settle on the inner rim of the lagoon.

How mud banks grow
Slowly, banks of mud build up. At low tide their tops appear in shallow tidal river mouths. Mud is rich in food for plants and their roots can burrow easily through soft, wet mud. So certain plants spring up on muddy estuary shores and offshore mudflats. As fresh mud lodges on these plants the mudbanks gradually grow above the level of all but the highest tide.

Such low mud islands can split a river mouth into many narrow channels. Where plants trap silt, this blocks some channel outlets. At low tide these channels form shallow pools of water, called salt pans.

In ways like this, rivers like the mighty Niger, Nile and Mississippi have built new tracts of land called *deltas* (after the Greek letter in the form of a triangle) out into the sea.

Shores as homes
Each kind of shore is home for a different set of sea creatures. You can find many species of worms and shellfish on muddy shores, for they can hide from enemies by burrowing. Shore mud is always wet and rich in nourishment, although the deeper

◄ A mangrove swamp at low tide reveals a mass of tree roots curving down into the mud with root 'knees' jutting up from the mud like woody spikes. Such roots do more than anchor the mangrove trees they sprout from. These breathing roots can take oxygen from air. They need to, for the waterlogged mud is almost starved of oxygen. Without their special roots, mangrove trees would suffocate.

▼ Mudskippers are tiny fishes that live in muddy mangrove swamps. Stiff fins help them walk and skip about on soft, wet mud. They can even climb up mangrove roots and trunks. At low tide, mudskippers are able to stay out of water for they can draw oxygen from the air as well as from water.

mud lacks oxygen.

Sandy shores are different. Sand holds less nourishment than mud, but shrimps, shellfish and many other creatures capable of tunnelling through sand find food and shelter here.

Rocky shores are not so hospitable. Only creatures that can burrow into solid rock or squeeze into crevices can actually hide themselves on a rocky shore. Most others rely on gripping the rock so tightly that they are not torn away by gales. Creatures with hard shells, limpets and barnacles, for example, survive for hours on rocks left high and dry by the retreating tide. Sea anemones and other soft-bodied creatures only survive in the tiny pools left in hollows of the rock. The water keeps them moist until the next rising tide covers the shore.

ISLANDS AND CORAL REEFS

▲ **Above** Fringing coral reefs grow just below the sea's surface around the island of Moorea in Polynesia. The reefs spread as new polyps build their stony homes against those of polyps that have died. There are hundreds of polyps in the branch of red coral (**top right**), but there are many millions in a big reef.

Millions of years ago vast chunks of land split up and moved apart to form the mighty island continents of Antarctica and Australia. But most islands are much smaller and appeared in other ways. The two main kinds are continental islands and oceanic islands.

Continental islands

Many of the largest islands lie near continents. Indeed these islands were once joined to the mainland. Take the British Isles, for instance. Its two biggest islands, Ireland and Great Britain, once formed part of mainland Europe. Sixteen thousand years ago you could have walked on dry land all the way from Ireland across Great Britain and into France. Later, the sea level rose and drowned low-lying land around the world. The rising waters cut off Ireland from Great Britain, then Great Britain from the rest of Europe. This also happened to Sundaland, a huge peninsula jutting out from mainland south-east Asia. All that remains of Sundaland today is a group of

islands. Borneo, Java and Sumatra are the largest.

Continental islands form where land is lost to the sea. But sea builds islands, too. Here and there waves heap up piles of sand until these rise above the sea. Low islands of this kind are known as *cays* or *keys*. Some lie off the southern tip of Florida. Others rest upon Australia's Great Barrier Reef.

Oceanic islands

Thousands of islands stand far from land. They rise from the deep floors of the Atlantic, Indian and Pacific oceans marking the summits of the ocean ridges. A few of these oceanic islands are sizeable – Iceland for example. But most are small. All appeared where volcanoes grew up from the ocean bed until they thrust above the sea.

Some oceanic islands are quite new. Lateika sprouted from the Pacific Ocean only in the 1970s. In 1963 sailors watched in amazement as fiery Surtsey was born off south-west Iceland: the sea boiled, then a vast heap of hot volcanic cinders rose above the water.

Most oceanic islands are much older than these two. The Hawaiian Islands probably grew one by one at million-year intervals. Tall volcanoes, some still active, crown Hawaii, the youngest of the group. But weather and waves have completely worn down the oldest Hawaiian islands.

Atolls and coral reefs

In time, many a volcanic island sinks deep below the waves. Often an *atoll* shows where this has happened. An atoll is a low ring of limy rock enclosing a lagoon. The rock is coral, made by billions of tiny living organisms called coral polyps.

Coral polyps thrive in warm, clear, sunlit salty water. But this water must be shallow. So new corals tends to build up on old dead coral as fast as the volcano that they stand on sinks below the sea. Particles of weed, sand, and other debris gradually fill up the spaces around the dead coral, forming a solid limestone rock.

Coral atolls began as reefs that ringed volcanic islands. Coral reefs grow also in shallow water off some mainland shores. The Great Barrier Reef stretches 2027km (1260 miles) just off the coast of north-east Australia. This reef forms the largest, longest coral mass on Earth.

coral island lagoon

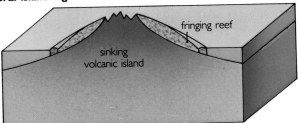

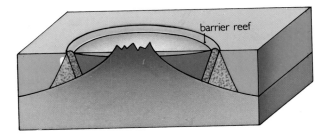

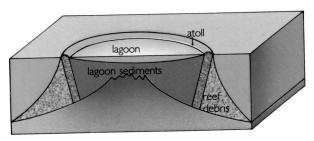

◄ Three diagrams show how a coral atoll forms. **Top** A coral fringing reef grows around the shore of a volcanic island. **Middle** Coral keeps on growing upward as the island sinks. The coral has become a barrier reef enclosing a lagoon around the island. **Bottom** The island has completely sunk. Now the coral forms an atoll enclosing only a lagoon.

▼ Coral reefs provide food and shelter for a wide variety of fish in warm, shallow tropical seas.

SEAWEEDS

Scientists believe that life on earth probably started in the sea. First came single living cells – tiny blobs of life of kinds too small to be seen without a microscope. From these evolved simple plants and animals, each made of thousands or millions of tiny cells. The first true plants were algae – the great group of simple plants including seaweeds.

You will see these strange saltwater plants when you visit a rocky shore. At low tide, many seaweeds seem to be just slippery, ugly strips, lying limply on rocks left bare by the retreating water. But when next high tide arrives, the sea buoys up their fronds. Then you can see how lovely many seaweeds are.

Although seaweeds may look a little like ordinary plants, they do not have true roots, stems and leaves. A seaweed's 'roots' are simply anchors that tether it to a rock, stone, shell or seaweed. Unlike true roots, these holdfasts do not absorb any nourishment for the plant.

From each holdfast rises a stem-like structure called a *stipe*. This can be stiff or floppy. It might support one or many leaf-like fronds, or stiff branchlets like teeth on a comb. At low tide, floppy stipes lie on the rocks. At high tide, when water buoys them up, the fronds make food with help from sunlight and chemicals in water. The fronds of bladderwrack even have tiny built-in balloons to help them float up as the tide comes in.

Not all seaweeds, however, have holdfasts. The Sargasso weed, living in the Sargasso Sea in the middle of the North Atlantic, is not anchored to anything. Instead, it floats on the surface in huge mats.

Different kinds of seaweed
All seaweeds need sunlight to make their food and all seaweeds belong to one or another of the three great groups: green, red and brown. These groups are related to the colours of sunlight and the depths to which they penetrate the sea. The red in sunlight travels to only just below the water's surface. So this is where you find green seaweeds – the kinds that need the red in sunlight. The blue in sunlight can

penetrate more than 100m (328ft). Red seaweeds can flourish at this gloomy depth because these use blue sunlight.

Brown seaweeds tend to need less light than green ones but more than red seaweeds. Brown often form dense underwater forests below the level of the greens but overshadowing the reds. One brown seaweed – the Pacific giant kelp – is the longest seaweed in the world. The fronds of one such plant can grow so long that you could wrap it right around a house.

How seaweeds survive
Because seaweeds need light, most grow in shallow water near the shore. But storm waves pound some coasts ferociously. Here, only the strongest holdfasts save seaweeds from being wrenched away and tossed up on the shore to die. In fact bladderwrack

▼ Bright green seaweeds grow in shallow inshore waters. A root-like holdfast anchors this specimen to coral on the Great Barrier Reef, off the north-east coast of Australia. Green seaweeds also grow in cooler waters all around the world.

holdfasts grip so well, that scientific tests have shown these seaweeds can survive all but the fiercest gales. Despite this, northern shores lose more than half their wracks in winter storms.

Seaweeds face other enemies besides the sea itself. Limpets and topshells damage them by nibbling and some fish graze on them. In some countries, people cook and eat seaweed and they are also harvested for industry, to be processed into fertilizers and gelatine.

But, meanwhile, new seaweeds sprout to take the place of those that die. Some grow from the leaves of adult plants. Some start life as runners – shoots sent out by the adult plants. Many seaweeds sprout from microscopic seed-like structures known as spores.

PLANKTON

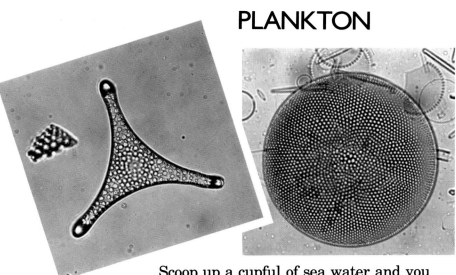

▲ These photographs show diatoms magnified many times. Diatoms are tiny one-celled algae with cell walls made in overlapping halves. The walls contain the glassy substance, silica.

Scoop up a cupful of sea water and you can trap thousands of living things too tiny to be seen without a microscope. These minute organisms are part of a mass of drifting plants and animals.

Scientists call these life-forms *plankton*, from a Greek word meaning 'wandering'. Instead of swimming around as strongly as an adult fish or squid, planktonic plants and animals drift at the mercy of the tides and currents. These organisms might seem small and insignificant, but they form foods on which most creatures in the sea depend. Many which live below the surface rise to the top at night. If disturbed, for example by a passing ship, they give off a radiant glow, a *phosphorescence*. This ghostly light has long been a source of wonder to seafarers and was the cause of many legends.

Phytoplankton

The main food providers are planktonic plants – the *phytoplankton*. For, unlike animals, plants manufacture food. Phytoplankton uses the energy in sunlight to produce food from water, carbon dioxide and minerals dissolved in the sea.

Much phytoplankton is made up of diatoms – tiny plants related to the seaweeds. A cupful of sea water is likely to contain 50,000 of these floating mini-plants encased in glass-like boxes largely made of silica. But oceans also teem with flagellates or 'whip bearers' – tiny organisms with built-in whips with which they propel themselves. Like animals, these specks of life can gobble solid food. Yet they contain *chlorophyll* the food-producing substance found only in green plants. And many have a skeleton of cellulose, a plant material. Flagellates come in many forms, for example tiny pots, masks or Chinese hats.

Zooplankton

Planktonic plants yield food for hordes of tiny planktonic animals – the zooplankton. Like planktonic plants, the foraminiferans and radiolarians which form a large part of the zooplankton, remain invisible unless seen through a microscope. In fact, radiolarians resemble little suns, with sticky 'rays' that help them trap their food. Foraminiferans have skeletons of calcium carbonate – the main ingredient in chalk. Indeed, the famous white cliffs of Dover, on England's south coast, are built up largely of the skeletons of foraminiferans that died and settled on an ancient sea bed which was later thrust above the water.

Zooplankton also swarms with the *larvae* of more familiar animals like crabs, jellyfish and fishes. But the larvae are very unlike their parents. A crab larva resembles a tail and legs poking from a spiky helmet, while the larvae of flatworms look like tiny, hairy balls.

Food chains and food pyramids

Creatures in the zooplankton feed on phytoplankton or each other. And both kinds of plankton form food for large, strongly swimming animals, like fishes, squids and whales. Each animal tends to

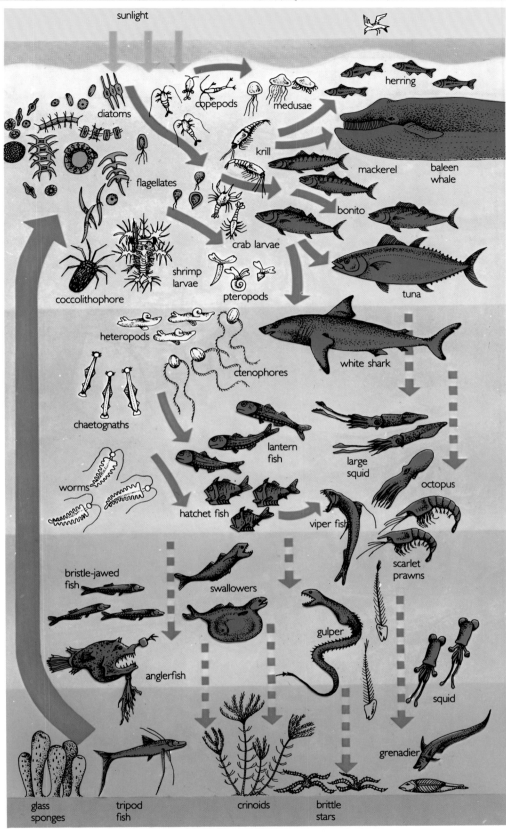

sunlight

diatoms

copepods

medusae

herring

krill

mackerel

baleen whale

flagellates

bonito

tuna

crab larvae

shrimp larvae

coccolithophore

pteropods

heteropods

white shark

ctenophores

chaetognaths

lantern fish

large squid

octopus

worms

hatchet fish

viper fish

scarlet prawns

bristle-jawed fish

swallowers

gulper

anglerfish

squid

grenadier

glass sponges

tripod fish

crinoids

brittle stars

◄ This picture shows how animals at every level in the sea depend for food on tiny planktonic plants and creatures living at the surface. Planktonic plants include the diatoms and the coccolithophores. With the plant-like flagellates, these form food for planktonic animals like copepods, medusas, krill and the larvae of shrimps and crabs. In turn these get gobbled up by nekton – strong swimmers such as fishes and squids.

phytoplankton

zooplankton

nekton

eat only certain kinds of food. For instance, phytoplankton forms food for tiny, shrimp-like animals called copepods. Copepods get gobbled up by herrings. A herring might be eaten by a cod. So planktonic plants and animals form links in chains made up of eaters and eaten.

In this way you can think of planktonic plants as the broad base of a mighty pyramid of food – a pyramid supporting just one large animal at the top. For instance, it might take 100,000 planktonic plants to feed 10,000 planktonic animals. In turn, these feed perhaps 1000 young herring, enough to nourish perhaps 10 cod or a single porpoise.

PLANT-LIKE ANIMALS

If you get the chance, peer closely into a rock pool at low tide. You may notice coloured blobs and 'blossoms' sprouting from the rocks. They look like plants, but are really simple kinds of animal.

Sponges

No animal could be much simpler than a sponge. Sponges have no head, mouth, limbs, or organs like a heart and lungs. Most are simply hollow blobs of jelly made of tiny cells and coloured green, red, brown or orange. Tiny glassy or horny needles stiffen a sponge's body and help to give it shape.

Water containing oxygen and minute particles of food enters a sponge through tiny holes in its sides. Then cells armed with whips lash the water through a hollow in the middle of the body. Here digestive cells absorb the food and oxygen and give off wastes. These squirt out used water through a single outlet like a miniature volcanic crater.

Baby sponges hatch from eggs inside their parent, which then squirts them out through its 'volcano' to start life in the open sea.

Scientists have carried out tests on sponges by pressing them through a special sieve. Sieving separates the cells that make up a sponge. But if they are left in a dish of water, the cells clump together again to build a new sponge, or maybe several sponges.

Coelenterates

Some of the most plant-like of all animals belong to the *coelenterates* or 'hollow gutted' group. The name comes from the pouch-shaped gut in which these creatures digest food. Coelenterates include sea anemones, coral polyps and jellyfish.

Most have a body shaped rather like a daisy. Indeed a sea anemone's tentacles look much like petals. But they are far more dangerous. Sea anemones use their tentacles to grasp small fishes or other passing prey. Many sea anemones can also sting and paralyze by shooting victims with long, poisoned threads. Once caught, a sea anemone stuffs the prey inside its mouth. This is just a hole at the top of the rubbery, hollow stalk that forms its body. The bottom of the stalk stays firmly attached to the rock. This way the sea anemone need not move around to catch its food.

Corals resemble small anemones, but usually live in groups on reefs. Each stony coral makes a tiny limestone cup in which it hides its body. Not all species of coral live on reefs, however. A few lead solitary lives on the cold dark floor of the oceanic abyss.

Sea anemones and corals spend their adult lives as so-called *polyps* fastened to the rocks. Jellyfish are different. Their eggs hatch into polyps. But these produce medusae – animals that look like tiny umbrellas made of jelly. Jellyfish medusae break free and drift about the surface of the sea. They catch prey with stinging tentacles that trail from their umbrellas.

Sea squirts

Adult sea squirts are among the strangest

▼ One of the 5,000 different kinds of sponge that are found in seas and oceans all over the world. They grow best, however, in the warm tropical seas.

◄ A pile of newly collected bath sponges drying on a beach before being cleaned and trimmed ready for sale.

◄ Sea anemones are simple animals that live by instinct. For instance, instinct makes them wrap their arms around their prey. Here a sea anemone pulls a fish inside its body cavity to be digested.

▼ Each of these 'stars on stalks' is a separate coral polyp. The whole group lives on the sea bed just below low-water level. Many kinds of coral polyp build stony coral cups into which they can shrink to hide from enemies.

of all the *sedentary* animals found in the sea. Young sea squirts look and swim like tadpoles. Then they glue themselves head-first to underwater rocks, and become blobs of water-squirting jelly. These take in water through one opening, extract nourishment from it, and squirt the water out through a second opening.

Sea squirts can be leathery and mud-coated, or soft, and shaded green or brown. They are in fact more complex than corals; besides a digestive system they have a heart pumping blood. It is possible to see their insides working because their outer 'tunic' is transparent. Unusually for any animal their covering is made mostly of cellulose, the main ingredient in plants. In fact sea squirts get their scientific name, tunicate, from their stiff outer tunic.

SEA WORMS

The earthworms that people dig up in a garden are just one of many kinds of worm. Some of the strangest live beneath the sea. Some sea worms are drab, others beautifully patterned. Some sprout tentacles; some are covered in a kind of hairy coat; some are too small to be seen with the naked eye, others grow to an incredible length.

Sea worms include members of four groups: bristle worms, flatworms, ribbon worms and roundworms.

No worms come in more variety than the bristle worms. The name comes from bristles growing from each segment or section of the body. Some bristle worms are active. Others make and live in tubes of sand and mud they cement around themselves.

▲ A fanworm spreads its feathery tentacles to trap food particles. Fanworms build themselves mud-and-mucus tubes sprouting from the sea bed. A frightened fanworm shrinks down inside its tube, pulling in its crown of tentacles.

▶ Roundworms are also known as nematodes, a word that means 'thread-like'. Many species of this group of worms are parasites that live in and feed on other animals or on plants.

▶ Bristle worms like these crawl or swim actively across the sea bed. Like an earthworm's body, theirs is divided into segments. The bristles jutting from each segment are easier to see than those on earthworms. Bristles can act as levers or paddles to help the bristleworm along.

Active bristle worms

To find active bristle worms you need search no deeper than the lower shore at low tide. Here, different bristle worms lurk under stones, lie buried in the sand, or prowl through weedy rock pools.

Ragworms are big and bright. They have a large head equipped with four eyes and several pairs of feelers. The creatures use their bodies' bristles to lever themselves along. Ragworms creep past underwater stones and seaweeds, hunting weaker worms or other prey, attacking them by unrolling a mouthpiece armed with curved black jaws. A big ragworm could nip your finger painfully.

Catworms look rather like ragworms but are more beautiful: gleaming like the mother-of-pearl that coats the inside of some sea shells. Unlike ragworms, catworms are scavengers; that is, they eat food that is already dead.

Paddleworms get their name from the pairs of flat 'paddles' that jut out from their bodies and help them swim.

Perhaps the strangest bristle worms are those belonging to the scale-worm family. A scale worm's bristles are really interlocking scales that guard its back. The sea-mouse looks very odd. This short, stubby worm has a hairy coat to keep sand grains from interfering with its breathing mechanism.

The stay-at-homes

For worms that roam in search of food a risk is that they might get caught and eaten by a fish or other predator. Tube worms lead lives designed to save them from this danger: they hide their bodies in some kind of cave.

Lugworms simply burrow in the sand. The sand mason worm builds a tunnel out of sand and stones, kept in place by sticky mucus manufactured by the worm. Peacock worms lurk in tubes of silt and mucus. Serpulid worms hide in tiny white tubes of rock-hard calcium carbonate glued to the surface of stones and seaweeds.

Serpulids, peacock worms and sand masons stay hidden in their tubes when low tide drains water from the shore. At high tide the first two thrust out feathery gills, while the sand mason sends tentacles writhing out across the beach. Between them, gills and tentacles trap particles of food. The lugworm scavenges for its food in the sand.

Flatworms and others

Flatworms are tiny. Many grow no longer than a fingernail. Most are brown or white. These flat, filmy worms seem to flow rather than slither over rocks and seaweed.

Ribbon worms are long, slim and slimy. Most are black, pink or red. They hide under stones and wrap themselves around the holdfasts of seaweeds. The species called the bootlace worm can claim to be the longest animal on Earth. Stretched out, one individual measured an amazing 55m (180ft).

Roundworms have rounded bodies, as their name suggests. The 'skin' is firm and smooth and they are pointed at the ends. Most are small. One kind lives in and feeds upon a brown seaweed, raising warty patches on the fronds.

ANIMALS WITH JOINTED LEGS

Arthropods (jointed-legged animals) outnumber all other sea beasts that have bodies made of many cells. The arthropod group includes land-dwelling flies and spiders; but most arthropods found in the sea are *crustaceans* – armoured animals with shells to guard their soft insides. All crustaceans breathe with gills and have two pairs of feelers. But different species have different kinds of jointed limbs according to whether they swim, walk, jump or do all three.

Some crustaceans are always surface swimmers; others mostly swim at lower levels. Yet others crawl across the bottom of the sea.

Swimming crustaceans

Tiny creatures called copepods live in surface waters all around the world. Some are smaller than a pencil dot, and the largest grow no longer than a thumbnail. Each has a very long pair of feelers and a long oval head and thorax (the next body section to the head). The tail is short and narrow. Five pairs of legs like paddles row the creature through the sea as it

◄ These beautiful shrimps come from the Straits of Messina between Italy and Sicily. The long, sensitive antennae are clearly visible and so are the shrimps' swimmerets. These are the pair of flattened limbs at the end of their bodies with which they propel themselves through the water.

◄ The sea anemone on which this shrimp is resting would sting and kill any other kind of shrimp. But shrimps of this species are safe. They make their homes among the tentacles of the anemone, safe from attack by their enemies.

browses on the tiny plants in plankton. Off Bermuda, three-quarters of all creatures fished up from the sea are copepods. Altogether the world probably holds more of these crustaceans than all other metazoan (many-celled) animals combined.

Shrimps and prawns are larger than the copepods. Prawns have two pairs of pincers, a projection called a rostrum jutting forward from the shell between the eyes, and a more rounded body than a shrimp. Shrimps grow only one pair of pincers, and have no rostrum. Both have special tail parts built for swimming: they can swim fast enough to dodge most enemies. But mostly they scavenge for food scraps on the sea bed. Indeed many shrimps spend much time burrowed in the sand.

Crabs and lobsters, larger relatives of the shrimps and prawns, also have ten legs joined to the thorax. Eight are walking legs, but the front pair have developed into powerful pincers for seizing prey and passing food to mouthparts armed with several pairs of jaws.

Crabs tend to have broad, flat bodies with a tail tucked forward beneath the thorax. Threatened crabs may wave their pincers or scuttle sideways to hide between rocks, or burrow in soft sand.

From time to time a crab outgrows its shell and moults. Then the crab is soft and unprotected until the new shell forms and hardens. That never happens to a hermit crab; it has no shell of its own but protects itself by living with its tender rear tucked in the empty shell of a whelk or other mollusc.

Lobsters are large, long-bodied crustaceans built much like hermit crabs. But they grow tough body armour and have a fan-shaped tail. Lobsters crawl across the sea bed in search of food scraps. If danger threatens, a lobster darts backward by a forward flick of the tail.

At the sea's edge

Perhaps barnacles are the strangest crustaceans of all. Only the young are free-swimming. Adults live attached to rocks, or on jetties and piling, and even on ships' hulls. Often you see acorn barnacles stuck on rocks at the sea's edge. At high tide their feathery jointed legs poke from their small, hard, white dome-like homes and grope for scraps of food. Stalked barnacles sprout from long, rubbery stalks attached to underwater wood or floating bottles.

The sea's edge is also home to small creatures that look rather like the woodlice found on land. Like woodlice, their bodies are built of segments guarded by hard, overlapping shields. The two main groups are isopods and amphipods. Isopods or 'equal footed' crustaceans have seven pairs of legs shaped much alike and used for walking. Amphipods or 'both footed' crustaceans tend to have three kinds of limbs: for walking, for swimming and for jumping.

Isopods include the gribble, a pest that gnaws holes in underwater timbers. The best-known amphipods are the sandhoppers that live under stones or seaweed lying on the beach. Disturb them and they hop about, then burrow on their sides into new hiding places.

◀ Stalked or goose barnacles resemble molluscs, but belong to the same group of animals as shrimps and crabs. Their shells open to let out 'legs' that fan water past each creature's mouth. With water comes life-giving oxygen and particles of food.

▶ The edible crab lives off Atlantic shores, especially if these are rocky. This large crab spawns in deep offshore waters, but in summer young ones often crawl inshore, hiding under stones in rock pools at low tide, until the sea fills the pools again.

SPINY SEA CREATURES

Imagine a headless animal with spines and feet sprouting from its arms. No, it is not a monster from a horror movie: you can see such creatures in rock pools at low tide. They are *echinoderms* – 'hedgehog skinned'. Starfish, brittle stars, sea cucumbers and sea urchins all belong to this strange and ancient group of animals.

Not all echinoderms are very spiny, but all lack heads, and they and their relatives all share the same main body plan. This consists of a central disc from which grow at least five arms or other body parts, slender 'tube feet' and hard limy plates below the skin. No other animals have this type of body.

Starfish and their kin
The most usual starfish have five long, leathery arms. Their relatives called sunstars can have as many as a dozen arms. The upper side of each arm is usually armed with tiny spines that move on *ball and socket joints*. Some of these spines are shaped like a bird's beak and can give an enemy a poisoned peck.

On the underneath of each arm are rows of tiny holes. From these peep scores of little tube feet that grow from bottle-like cavities filled with water. When muscles squeeze these bottles, water squirts into the tube feet, making them lengthen. But when water flows back into the bottles the feet tips act as suckers. They grip a rock so firmly that even storm waves cannot tear a starfish loose.

A starfish's mouth is in the middle of the lower surface of the body. Small sea creatures, which are swallowed whole, are its main food. But starfish also eat cockles. To deal with these thick-shelled *molluscs* the starfish climbs astride and grips the two halves of the cockle's shell, slowly pulling them apart. Then the attacker pushes its stomach out through its mouth and into the cockle. There, the starfish's stomach starts digesting the cockle's soft, unprotected flesh.

Brittlestars have, as their name suggests, long and brittle arms. But, like starfish, brittlestars can regrow arms snapped off by enemies or accidents.

Starfish shed body waste and eggs from a hole in the middle of the top of the central disc.

Sea urchins and sand dollars
Imagine the arms of a starfish bent upwards to meet above its central disc and the gaps between them filled in. This shows that the round sea urchin is similar to the five-rayed starfish, although they do not look much alike.

Sea urchins resemble pin-cushions bristling with pins. In fact the sharp ends of their spines stick out from a hard, usually dome-shaped, shell that guards each urchin's body. From the mouth beneath the middle of the shell five bands containing rows of tiny holes run upward to the top. These bands correspond to the five arms of the starfish. The urchin's long slim tube feet emerge from these holes. It moves on these feet, helped along by the spines. The feet tether it to rock, and can also grope around on the sea bed searching for food particles. But many urchins eat more solid meals. With the sharp teeth that edge the mouth beneath the body they can munch seaweed or tube worms.

Sand dollars are closely related to sea

▲ The sea urchin is well protected against its enemies – the sharp spines covering it grow from a hard protective shell.

▲ A much-magnified brittle star larva looks nothing like the adult animal it will become. Each side of the larva's body matches the other. But an adult brittle star has a central body that sprouts five identical arms.

▶ This view shows how a brittlestar's arms sprout from its central disc. You can clearly see the forest of tube feet projecting from each arm. But the arms themselves are too long to fit completely into the photograph.

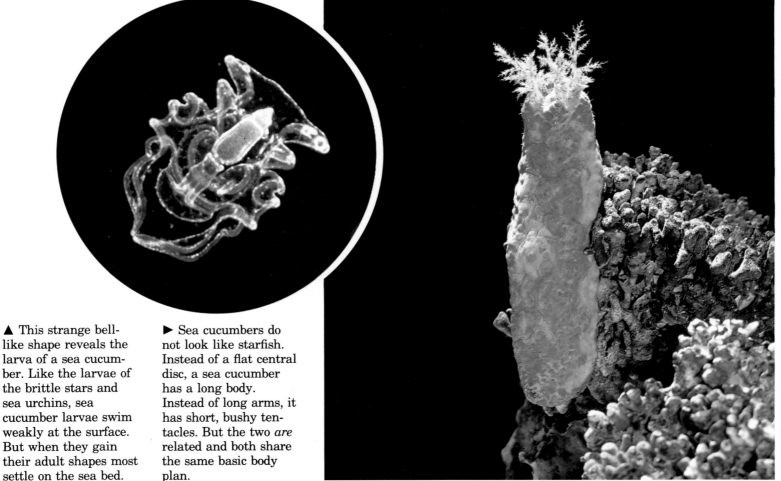

▲ This strange bell-like shape reveals the larva of a sea cucumber. Like the larvae of the brittle stars and sea urchins, sea cucumber larvae swim weakly at the surface. But when they gain their adult shapes most settle on the sea bed.

▶ Sea cucumbers do not look like starfish. Instead of a flat central disc, a sea cucumber has a long body. Instead of long arms, it has short, bushy tentacles. But the two *are* related and both share the same basic body plan.

urchins. They live in the sandy floor of the sea. Long arms, or even spikes, would be a disadvantage here, so the sand dollar has become flattened, like a coin, and has a broad disc with no arms.

Sea cucumbers

Many sea cucumbers resemble small, squat cucumbers or gherkins. At first glance their longish body plan is quite unlike that of a sea urchin or starfish. Yet sea cucumbers usually have five bands of tube feet running down the body, and a mouth at one end. The bush of tentacles around the mouth helps the creature feed.

Sea cucumbers might seem poorly defended, apart from their tough skins. But they have a secret weapon. If a lobster or other enemy attacks, a sea cucumber squirts most of its insides out through its anus – the hole at the end opposite the mouth. The creature also shoots out sticky threads. While these entangle or confuse the lobster, the sea cucumber escapes. Within a fortnight it will grow a new set of 'insides' and so be able to defend itself in this way again.

SOFT-BODIED CREATURES

The pretty sea shells you can find cast up on the shore once guarded the soft bodies of the animals that lived inside them. The commonest type of such creatures are called *molluscs* from the Latin word for 'soft'. The most familiar marine molluscs are clams, oysters, octopuses and squids.

Gastropod and bivalve molluscs

The molluscs most of us know best are those garden pests the snails and slugs. Both are gastropods – a term that comes from the Latin word meaning 'stomach footed'. Gastropods have one large fleshy foot on which they crawl around. Above the foot lie other body organs. There is also a so-called 'mantle' of tissue that manufactures the shell of those gastropods, such as snails, that have shells. Unlike some other molluscs, gastropods have a head and eyes and most hide inside a single shell.

Most species live in the sea. Sea snails include the dogwhelks and topshells.

▲ Orange spikes jut from a sea urchin that is crawling slowly over living coral polyps. But some of the sea urchin's tube feet grip the glass front of the aquarium containing it. These feet show as thin, white threads. Each ends in a sucker smaller than a pinhead.

These creatures have a body joined to a column running up through the middle of a spiral shell. If danger threatens, a sea snail pulls its foot inside its shell. A hard, tough plug on the foot blocks the shell's doorway and so helps to keep out predators. But some sea snails are flesh-eaters. They can drill holes through other molluscs' shells and feed upon the meat inside.

Many sea snails, though, browse on plants. For instance, limpets use their horny 'tongues' to rasp seaweed off rocks. At low tide they clamp their low, pointed shells tightly against a rocky surface. This helps them trap enough water to stop their bodies drying up before the tide creeps in and moistens them again.

Just as slugs are shell-less snails, so sea slugs are shell-less sea snails. Sea slugs are often beautifully coloured and some sprout showy frills. Six kinds are pictured on the next two pages.

Bivalves are headless molluscs protected

▲ This mollusc lives inside a single shell, so the creature is a gastropod. From its soft body project a pair of 'feelers' that sense touch, light and scent.

▼ This sea slug's 'tentacles' resemble those of the sea anemones it preys upon. The creature smothers the anemone's stinging tentacles with slime, then swallows them. The stinging cells pass into the 'tentacles' on the sea slug's back. There they can sting any enemy attacking the sea slug.

by a shell with two hinged valves or halves. Bivalves do not need to move much to find food. Instead, they suck water in through a tube called a siphon, and extract food particles from it. Another siphon squirts out water and body waste. Some bivalves have long inlet siphons that they can use like an elephant's trunk, sucking scraps of food from the sea bed.

Bivalves such as razor shells burrow in soft sand. But mussels use a web of threads to help them cling onto rocks. Some other bivalves bore tunnels into wood or limestone.

Surprisingly, bivalves called scallops can jet through water at high speed. They

have a row of very primitive 'eyes' on the rim of the mantle. When a starfish, for example, comes near, they snap their shells to force water out in one direction. This sends the scallops fast the other way, so avoiding capture.

Cephalopods and chitons
Cephalopods get their name from the Greek words meaning 'head footed'. This group of molluscs includes the squid, octopus and cuttlefish. Each has a large head, big eyes and well-developed brain. From the head sprout tentacles for gripping prey. The squids and cuttlefish have only a thin horny 'shell' embedded in their body and the octopus has none.

These creatures can swim in one direction by squirting water the opposite way through a siphon. Squids and octopuses can also squirt out clouds of ink to confuse an enemy so that they can make a quick getaway.

Chitons are yet another major group of molluscs. They resemble the land woodlice, for eight overlapping plates protect each chiton's little body, and it curls up if disturbed. Like limpets, chitons cling tightly to the rocks on which they browse.

▼ This sea slug browses on green seaweeds. It swallows but does not digest their chloroplasts – tiny units containing a food-producing chemical called chlorophyll. The chloroplasts travel down the sea slug's gut then into dead-end tubes that lead off to the sides. There, the chloroplasts continue making starchy foods. The sea slug digests these and they give it energy.

► This is another seaweed-eating sea slug. Like two others on these pages it bears a bushy tuft of tentacles that serve as gills. Such tentacles grow in a ring around the creature's anus, a hole from which it lets out body waste.

◄ This sea slug is knobbly and has a black, white and yellow pattern that breaks up its shape. Sea slugs patterned in this way can be surprisingly difficult to see against the seabed surfaces on which they live and feed. Many sea slugs depend on camouflage to hide them from their enemies.

▲ Feathery 'tentacles' sprout from this sea slug's back. They look like decoration, but in fact are gills through which the creature breathes. Sea slugs with gills exposed like this belong to the main sea slug group – nudibranchs. (The name means 'naked gills'.) The slug is pictured here much larger than life. Most nudibranchs are no longer than the end joint of a man's thumb.

4 ANIMALS WITH BACKBONES

SHARKS AND RAYS

The sea creatures so far mentioned lack a
backbone. But the sea provides a home for
backboned animals as well: fishes,
mammals, birds and reptiles. A backbone
helps to give the body shape and strength
and provides an anchorage for muscles. It
forms part of an internal (inside) skeleton
that grows to keep pace with the rest of
the body. So backboned animals do not
moult their skeletons as they grow, as
crabs must shed their shells from time to
time.

The 'gristle' fish

By far the most abundant backboned
creatures in the sea are fish. But not all
fish have a bony skeleton. The skeletons
of sharks and rays are made of a softer,
springier material called cartilage or
gristle. (Your own body contains some
cartilage: you can feel cartilage inside the
tip of your nose.)

There are other differences between
sharks and bony fishes. Instead of smooth,
flat scales, a shark's body is covered by
skin so rough that craftsmen once used it
as a kind of sandpaper. Like bony fishes,
sharks breathe out through *gills* behind
the head, but sharks' gills show up as
several slits, for they lack the flap of scaly
skin that hides a bony fish's gills. Then,
too, sharks and rays have no swim

bladder to control their level in the sea. Most must keep on swimming or they will sink to the sea bed.

Tigers of the deep

Sharks are mostly streamlined killers. They have long, torpedo-shaped bodies, tapered at both ends. Their mouths are armed with rows of sharp teeth just right for slicing flesh. Sharks' teeth grow in rows, and each row moves gradually forward, so as the front teeth wear out, teeth that were originally at the back take their place. Sharks have a keen sense of smell and sight, and they can sense vibrations made by other creatures in the water. All this helps them find and snap up fish and other prey.

Many tales tell of sharks attacking shipwrecked sailors. The great white shark is big and fierce enough to chop off an arm or leg with just one bite. But not all sharks are dangerous to man. The whale shark, which can grow to 18m (60ft) and is the world's largest fish, feeds harmlessly on plankton. Another shark, the wobbegong, that is found in the seas round Australia, lives on the sea bed and eats molluscs.

Rays and ratfishes

Rays are 'gristle fishes' with broad bodies, flattened from top to bottom. They 'swim' by flapping gracefully through water like strange birds. But many spend much time lying on the ocean floor, where their dark backs camouflage them from enemies. These bottom-dwellers generally have broad, flat teeth, designed for crunching up the shellfish on which they feed.

In some shallow seas, stingrays lurk on the sandy floors of shallow bays. If trodden on, a stingray lashes out with a tail armed with a sharp spine, poisonous enough to kill small animals. A relative, the torpedo or electric ray, can give off an electric shock powerful enough to stun a man.

The largest rays are the devil rays or mantas, which can grow to 6m (20ft) across. Unlike most of their relatives, mantas cruise along the surface, eating plankton and small fishes. But they are harmless to people and look far more terrifying than they are.

Some sharks and rays lay eggs protected by a long, tough, flattish case. These are the so-called mermaids' purses you can sometimes find washed up on the shore.

The ratfishes, or chimaeras, a third group of 'gristle fish', are shaped rather like tadpoles. They have stout bodies that taper to a long and very slender tail. The head is big and pointed with large eyes. The teeth have joined to form broad, sharp chisels. A strange prickly hook juts forward from the male chimaera's head, perhaps to clasp a female during courtship. Chimaeras grow about 1m (3ft) long, and most live near the bottom of the sea.

▲ What a contrast this tasselled wobbegong shark is to the streamlined white-tip reef shark (**opposite**). This is because it catches its food by lying, well camouflaged, on the sea bed waiting to grab fish as they swim past.

▼ Rays such as this thornback spend their lives lying hidden in or on the seabed sand or swimming slowly just above it. These fishes largely prey on crabs and other bottom dwellers.

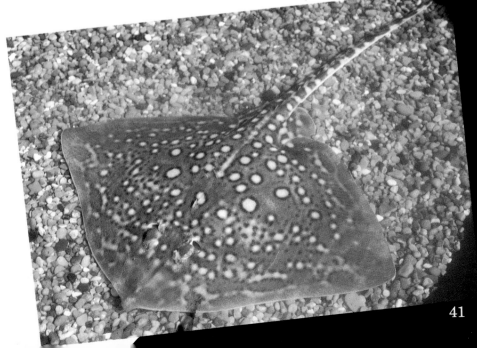

BONY FISH

Most of the world's 30,000 kinds of fish have skeletons of bone, and many live in seas or oceans. The smallest species is a goby no longer than a thumbnail. In fact it is the smallest backboned animal of any kind. The largest bony fish is the ocean sunfish, a strange creature flattened from side to side and shaped as a gigantic disc with fins. An ocean sunfish can weigh 2 tonnes or more. But the Russian sturgeon is the longest bony fish – some measure 8m (26ft).

How fish live

Like sharks and rays, bony fish are especially designed to live in water. They breathe by taking mouthfuls of water and gathering the oxygen in it with filters known as gills. Because a sea fish's tissues are less salty than the sea around, water continually seeps out from its body to the sea. The fish makes up this loss by drinking in more water. Special cells inside the fish help to remove some of this water's saltiness.

Like sharks, bony fish have fins that help them steer and keep their balance. Many have a powerful tail that they sweep from side to side to help thrust their bodies through the water. Eyes, nostrils and a line of sense cells along each side of the body help bony fish find food and warn them of danger.

At times, most fish must swim fast to catch agile prey or to escape a speedy predator. Some can swim very fast indeed. The sailfish can reach 100kph (62mph) when chased by fishermen. The little flying fish can even swim fast enough to take off and glide far through the air on fins that serve as wings. Such fish as these tend to have a particularly streamlined shape.

Fish defences

Even speedy swimmers have camouflage that helps them to hide from their enemies. Fish living at the surface are silvery. Birds and other fish cannot easily pick them out against the sparkling waves and bright surface layers of water. Just under the surface are fish, such as tuna and mackerel, with pale bellies and mottled bluish backs. With this colouring, such fish are difficult to see either from above or from below. In shallow waters bottom-dwelling fish move slowly and are often brownish and spotted with markings that echo the pebbles or sand where they live. Flatfish like the plaice and sole can burrow in soft sand until you can see only their eyes watching out for enemies. The huge moray eel also hides by day, tucking its body into an underwater cave or crevice.

Fish living in the brightly-lit waters around coral reefs, are themselves the most brilliantly coloured swimmers. Some use this coloration as camouflage, but others flaunt their stripes, and rely for defence on sharp teeth or spines, or the fact that they are extremely poisonous to eat. The lionfish and the dragonfish are, as you would expect from their names, quite able to defend themselves in this way. Deep sea fish, living in near or total darkness, are usually black or red. (Red looks black when it is far below the surface.)

Finding food

Just as different fish have different defences, so they have many ways of catching food. Those slender-bodied hunters, the barracuda, have powerful jaws bristling with teeth for seizing fish smaller than themselves. A swordfish uses the long 'sword' jutting from its head to

▼ This plaice is blotched and shaded like the pebbles that it lies on. The fish's camouflage conceals it from predators. Plaice are flattened from side to side, and lie with one side uppermost. Both eyes lie facing upward from that side.

▲ Mackerel, swimming near the surface, feed largely on tiny animals in plankton. Seen from beneath, a mackerel's silvery belly blends with the bright surface of the sea. From above, its dark back merges with the gloomy depths below. Despite their camouflage, many mackerel fall prey to big flesh-eating fish.

▶ This little creature has a head shaped like a horse's, and bony rings that produce ridges jutting from its body, but it is, in fact, a fish. Sea horses swim upright, using tiny fins to drive themselves along. This one has curled its tail around a piece of coral.

slash at shoals of small fish. The little shark remora uses a sucker under its head to glue itself onto a shark. The remora eats small parasites that live on the shark, but swims free to gobble scraps left when the shark has made a kill.

The parrot fish has even stranger feeding habits. This creature has a mouth ending in a kind of 'parrot's beak', and uses it to snip off bits of growing coral. The fish crunches up the coral and digests the juicy coral polyps hiding in it.

DWELLERS IN THE DEPTHS

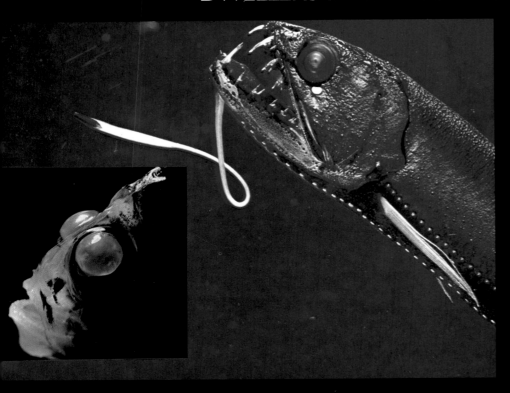

◄ *Astronesthes* is a sharp-fanged, slender-bodied fish living deep below the ocean's surface. Rows of tiny lights illuminate its body in the darkness. From its lower jaw curls a glowing fleshy strip. Small fish are attracted by this lure.

► Snipe eels live deep down in temperate and tropical oceans. Sometimes, especially at night, they swim up to the surface. Snipe eels have huge appetites. Scientists caught one that had swallowed a snipe eel as big as itself.

▲ The huge eyes of this hatchet fish can rotate in their sockets. Deep-sea fish with large eyes can detect pinpoints of light on other fishes' bodies. This helps individuals to find mates and avoid enemies.

Most marine plants and animals live in the sunlit upper level of the sea. It is only here that plants find light enough for growth, and almost all sea animals depend on plants for food either directly or indirectly.

Few plants survive as far down as 180m (600ft) for this is the ocean's twilight zone. Below this all is always black as night. Yet creatures manage to survive even in these gloomy depths.

Deep-sea animals find food in one of three main ways. At night, lantern fishes, prawns and squids swim up to the surface to feed on tiny creatures in the plankton. Many other deep-sea creatures eat each other, or prey upon the lantern fishes, squids and prawns. Yet other deep-sea dwellers eat dead animals and plants drifting from the surface to the sea bed.

Lights beneath the sea

Many deep-sea fishes glow with rows of lights. For instance, lantern fishes have two rows along the bottom of the body and on the head, and more lights on the tail. Perhaps these attract the tiny prey they eat. Sharp-jawed, slender little fish known as stomiatoids have rows of glowing 'buttons' on their bodies. Some individuals shine with many thousand tiny lamps. A few fish have silvery sides –

mirrors for reflecting light. Shiny body surfaces and glowing lights could serve several purposes: they might help fish of one species to find a mate. They might attract prey. They might also confuse a predator.

Lures and traps

Deep, deep down, food becomes so scarce that fish cannot waste energy in active hunting, or feeding a large body. So most are small and simply lie in wait for food. Gulpers are a good example. Most of a gulper's weak, flabby body seems to be a mouth shaped like a roomy bag. Some gulpers have a reddish light shining from the whip-like tail. Probably the light lures other fish to come near. The gulper seems to lie still until its senses that its victim is in range. Then the creature's jaws gape wide and close around the prey.

But among all fishing fish the deep-sea anglers stand out. Most are lumpy, pear-shaped fish no larger than a man's fist. Their huge heads have large jaws bristling with long, curved, spiky fangs. A long 'fishing line' sprouts from the deep-sea angler's head. This line ends in a fleshy glowing lump that serves as bait. A deep-sea angler floats almost motionless deep down. When a fish comes up to take the bait, the angler's mouth yawns open and sucks the victim in.

The deep-sea floor

Life thrives even on the lowest levels of the ocean floor. There, shrimps and flatfish swim. The strangely shaped tripod fish rests on soft mud without sinking, thanks to three long fin rays that support it like a tripod. Most creatures of the deep-sea floor are scavengers, finding nourishment by sucking in dead animal remains or droppings.

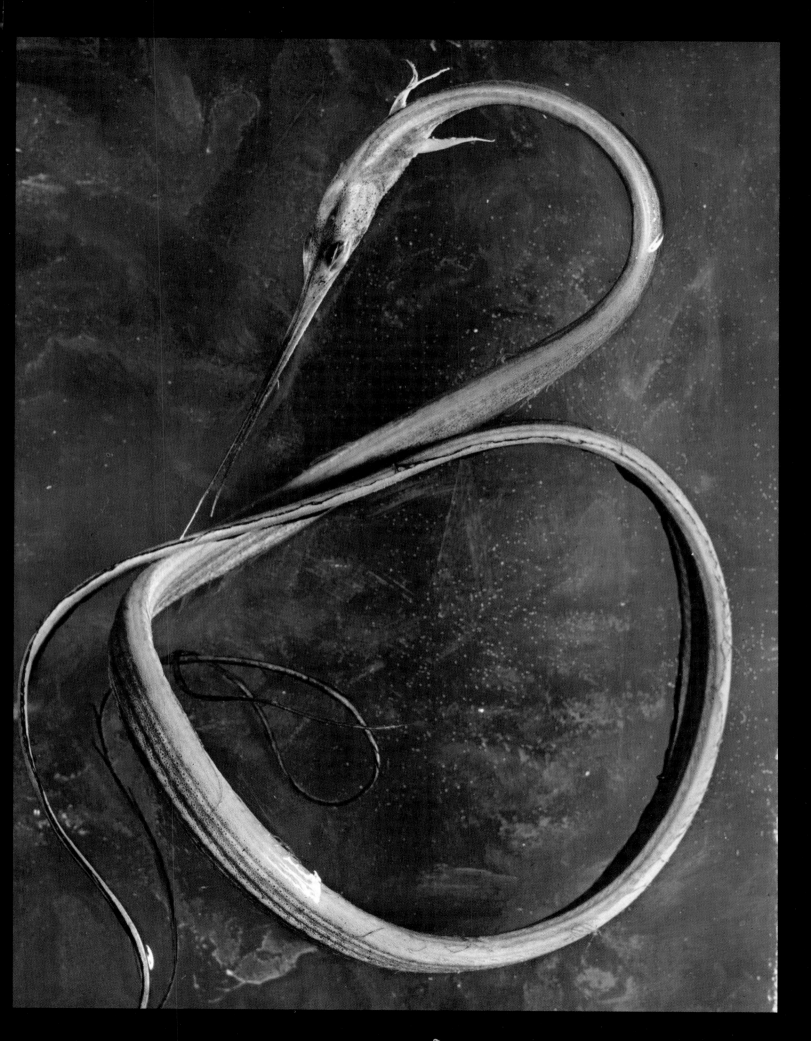

SEALS AND POLAR BEARS

▲ Hooded seals, such as this mother and her pup, are found particularly among the ice floes of the Greenland Sea and the Gulf of St Lawrence in North America.

Unlike fish, mammals are warm-blooded animals with lungs, not gills, and cannot breath below the water. Yet millions of years ago some mammals took to living in the sea. Their descendants are today's sea mammals such as seals and whales.

Seals

Seals are heavy-bodied beasts with limbs that have evolved as flippers. All seals have thick layers of fat or dense fur to stop their bodies chilling in cold water or air. Many swim happily in water cold enough to kill a man in minutes. Seals swim superbly as they hunt for fish or shellfish. Some can dive to great depths and stay down a long while. Hooded and harp seals, for example, often plunge 1000m (3300ft) in search of food on the sea bed. These seals can stay down for half an hour before they must come up to

breathe. Most seals only come ashore to bask, breed or moult.

There are three main types of seal: eared seals, earless seals and walruses. Eared seals, as their name suggests, have ear flaps. On land they can bring their hindlimbs forward and lift their bodies off the ground, moving quite fast if threatened. Strong front limbs, thick body fat and springy ribs protect them from injury as they scramble over rocks.

There are two main kinds of eared seal: sea lions and fur seals. Sea lions include the largest eared seals. Steller's sea lion bulls grow nearly 4m (13ft) long and weigh up to one tonne. The females are much shorter and two-thirds lighter. These sea lions live near coasts around the North Pacific.

Fur seals have thick coats of fine hair. This helps to keep them warm in the cold waters where most fur seals live. At breeding time, northern fur seals gather in huge seashore 'rookeries'. From one island hilltop in the Bering Sea scientists have counted 100,000 of them. Nowhere else on Earth could you see so many large mammals at one time and place. The adult bulls arrive at the rookeries first, hauling themselves ashore in May or June to fight one another for a stretch of beach. Then, as the cows arrive, each winner gathers about 40 to form a harem. Soon each cow gives birth to a pup which grows fast. By November the young are ready to leave their mothers and go to sea.

Earless seals lack ear flaps, and have weak, short forelimbs. On land their hindlimbs always trail behind and they cannot lift their bodies off the ground. Instead, they hump along the beach in a most ungainly way. The smallest earless seal is the ringed seal, an Arctic mammal measuring only 1.4m (4½ft). The largest earless seal, and the largest seal of any kind, is the southern elephant seal. Males can grow to 6.4m (21ft) or more and weigh three or four tonnes. Of all sea mammals, only whales grow larger.

The walrus is the only species in its family, and lives only in cold northern waters. A heavy beast, an adult walrus can weigh over a tonne. The two long tusks that jut down from the upper jaw are used to punch breathing holes in sea ice and to help the walrus haul itself onto ice floes.

The polar bear
Eared seals probably evolved from ancestors related to bears. We think of bears as land mammals, but polar bears spend much time on and in the sea. These huge white hunters roam the shores and islands of the Arctic Ocean, but can swim 32km (20 miles) or more to find new feeding grounds. Seals form their main prey. A polar bear creeps up on a seal basking on a slab of floating ice, then charges before its victim can plunge into the water. Polar bears also wait in ambush by seals' breathing holes kept open through sea ice. When a seal swims up to breathe, a swift blow from the bear's paw drags it to the surface.

Polar bears lead solitary lives, for only females and their young hunt together.

▼ The thick coat of the polar bear protects it against the severe cold of the Arctic winters. A polar bear will wait for hours on the ice to catch a seal as it surfaces to breathe.

WHALES

Seals spend most of their lives at sea; whales never come ashore. As a result a whale's body has evolved to look more like a fish's. But where a fish's tail fin is flat from side to side, a whale's tail flukes are flat from top to bottom. Whales beat their flukes up and down to drive their bodies forward through water. They steer and balance with flipper-shaped forelimbs. Some also have a fin that juts up from the back to help to keep them upright. Whales usually swim in groups called schools or herds.

Beneath a whale's skin lies a thick layer of fat or blubber. By trapping body heat, this helps to keep the whale warm. Blubber also provides a stored energy supply.

Whales must swim to the surface to breathe. Newborn calves are often helped by adults, which nudge them upwards. Whales breathe through a blowhole in the head. Moisture in the air they breathe out condenses as a fine spray that looks like a fountain. The height, width and angle of this 'spout' can help an expert to identify the kind of whale that made it.

Toothed whales
All whales belong to one of two main groups: toothed and baleen whales. Toothed whales include dolphins, porpoises and sperm whales. They range from small, streamlined creatures like the man-length harbour porpoise up to the sperm whale which measures up to 18m (60ft).

Toothed whales are famous for making underwater sounds and listening to the echoes bounced back off underwater objects. This helps the whales to track down fish or other prey; it also helps them avoid obstacles like rocks.

Toothed whales use their peg-shaped teeth for seizing sizeable fish, squid or other animals. And the sperm whale can plunge 2200m (7200ft) in search of squid. An oil-filled 'buoyancy tank' built into this whale's enormous head enables it to sink or rise at will.

Whales can hold their breath for such long periods partly because they can slow their heart beat. They also have remarkably efficient ways of storing oxygen and concentrating blood where it is needed most at any particular time.

Baleen whales
The baleen whales get their name from the horny plates of baleen or whalebone with frayed edges hanging from the rim of the upper jaw. These 'combs' form sieves to help the whales feed. To take a meal, a baleen whale swims open-mouthed through shoals of fish or swarms of tiny shrimp-like creatures. When the whale shuts its mouth its tongue squeezes water out through the baleen fringe, trapping the animals it will eat inside.

The blue whale, the largest baleen whale, is also the largest living animal. This enormous animal can grow as much as 33.6m (110ft) long, and weigh 170 tonnes.

The grey whale, another species of baleen whale, makes longer regular

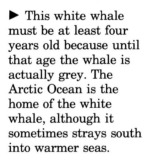

▶ This white whale must be at least four years old because until that age the whale is actually grey. The Arctic Ocean is the home of the white whale, although it sometimes strays south into warmer seas.

migrations than any other mammal. Each year adults swim south from Arctic waters to the Gulf of California to breed. Then adults with their young swim back north to their feeding grounds. The round trip can be 18,000km (11,250 miles).

◄ Open-mouthed, this sea mammal reveals the peg-shaped teeth that show it to be a toothed whale. This is a dolphin, one of the smallest of whales.

Dolphins are harmless to man, but a killer whale's large teeth and huge jaws could inflict terrible injury. But both whales can be tamed.

▼ Dolphins leaping out of the water. Some swim and leap for hours ahead of ships crossing an ocean. Animals that enjoy playing like this tend to be more intelligent than most. Scientists know that dolphins can communicate with each other. They can also be taught many circus tricks.

BIRDS AND REPTILES

Hundreds of kinds of birds and a few kinds of reptiles use the ocean as a larder, and the seashore as a feeding ground or nursery.

Birds of the open sea

Seabirds such as gulls and albatrosses are superbly shaped for flying without effort over waves. Both have long, narrow wings rather like a glider's. Indeed the wandering albatross has longer wings than any other bird. This seabird spends almost all its life gliding on the winds that always blow around Antarctica. An albatross can fly for hours just above the troughs and crests of waves, without a single wing flap. It gains speed by swooping downward with the wind, then turns against the wind to climb. Albatrosses steer with their feet, which jut out well beyond the tail.

Such seabirds feed on creatures in the sea below. Some seabirds are particularly good at catching fish. Among these experts are the terns – graceful birds with slender, pointed wings. Terns hover over the sea, then plunge in just deep enough to snatch up small fish swimming near the surface. Brown pelicans, gannets and cormorants dive deeper, and catch larger prey. Near coasts, where the sea is shallow, sea ducks will plunge to the very bottom to feed on shrimps, worms or crabs. Perhaps the strangest meals are those of the small wading birds called red phalaropes. These land on whales resting at the surface, and eat whale lice, little parasites that feed upon the monsters' bodies.

Birds on the shore

Seashores team with food for long-legged wading birds. Oystercatchers use their chisel-shaped beaks to open mussels. Other wading birds with slender beaks probe sand and mud for shellfish, worms and small crustaceans. Ringed plovers have short beaks and feed on creatures that live in shallow burrows.

Cliffs and sandy beaches provide nesting grounds for many birds that find food in the sea or on the shore. Gulls, gannets, guillemots and razorbills nest on cliff ledges where eggs and chicks are safe from predators such as rats and foxes. Certain terns, plovers and gulls prefer low, sandy or shingly shores. Such birds tend to lay eggs blotched or speckled to match the sand and pebbles. This camouflage hides eggs from creatures that would eat them. Also, terns and other seabirds nest in colonies. The parents gang up to dive-bomb and drive off dogs or people who come too near.

Reptiles and the sea

Several kinds of lizard live on seashores. One gecko even catches crabs. Certain reptiles live largely in the sea. Estuarine crocodiles are the world's largest crocodiles and can grow up to 9m (30ft) in length. They swim far from shore in the Indian and Pacific oceans. On the Pacific's Galápagos Islands are found large, dark lizards called marine iguanas. Each day they dive beneath the sea to browse on seaweeds. Tropical seas are homes to sea snakes, too. These poisonous, fish-hunting reptiles have flattened tails to help them swim.

Probably the reptile most suited for life at sea is the marine turtle, with its long, flat forelimbs that help it travel fast through the water. The short, broad hindlimbs serve as rudders. Marine turtles live in warm seas and oceans. Some browse on underwater plants. Others feed on animals like jellyfish and squid. All come ashore to breed. Each

▼ This illustration shows the salt glands in a herring gull. This bird drinks salty sea water. Salt glands above its eyes prevent too much salt collecting in the body. They draw salt from the blood, and let it out in a special solution. This flows through a tube, then drips from the bird's beak.

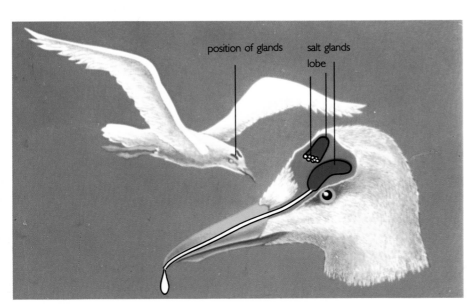

position of glands   salt glands lobe

◀ Gannets nest on sea cliffs in colonies of hundreds of birds. These birds spend their lives fishing at sea. They only gather on coasts to breed. If space there is scarce, individuals fight fiercely for nest sites little larger than their own bodies.

female digs a deep hole with her flippers. She lays eggs in the hole, then covers them with sand, and leaves them for the Sun to hatch. Months later, baby turtles struggle free and race down to the sea.

Sea turtles range in size from the ridley to the leatherback: ridleys measure 1m (3ft) or less, leatherbacks can grow to nearly 3m (10ft) and weigh more than half a tonne.

▶ This green turtle is swimming just below the sea's surface. It hatched from one of scores of eggs as big as a billiard ball, laid in a hole scooped out of some sandy, tropical beach. Of every 100 turtle hatchlings, only one may reach the sea. Birds, dogs, crabs and people eat the rest.

5 MAN AND THE SEA

▲ The *Queen Elizabeth 2* is a cruise liner, it has four restaurants, seven bars, plus cinemas, theatres and gymnasiums, all arranged on 13 decks. One thousand crewmen run the ship, which holds 1400 passengers. Once, all passengers crossed oceans by ship. Now most fly.

▶ The wheelhouse is the control centre of a ship. The sailor at the wheel steers with help from navigation instruments. In front of him are a magnetic compass and gyrocompass. To his right is a radar receiver. An officer can telephone orders instantly to crew members in distant parts of the ship.

OCEAN HIGHWAYS

Once the ocean was a barrier to travel. Now oceans serve as highways, enabling passengers and goods to travel around the world. Long ago, people could only gaze across the sea and wonder what lay beyond. Yet as early as 40,000 years ago, Stone Age adventurers had already reached Australia, most likely by canoe, and New Zealand and the Pacific Islands had been inhabited long before Europeans reached them in the eighteenth century. By 4500 years ago, sailors had ships that sailed the Mediterranean Sea.

For thousands of years, though, all ocean-going ships were small, built of wood and only powered by oar or sail. Their sailors knew the winds and currents in the area, yet voyages out of sight of land were always perilous and wherever possible they kept close to the coast, or sailed from one island to the next. Even so, storms sank many thousands of fragile craft.

It has only been possible to build big, safe, speedy ocean-going ships since the last century. Modern ships have metal hulls that can be built to almost any size. The world's largest vessel is a supertanker capable of carrying a load of over 560,000 tonnes. This craft is about four soccer pitches long, and broader than six tennis courts laid side by side. Yet the ship only needs a small crew. Powerful engines or motors spin screws that drive such ocean-going ships along.

Each day cargo ships carry huge quantities of oil from oil wells in the Middle East to nations around the world. Bulk carriers transport massive loads of raw materials like iron ore from Australia to countries like Japan. From Argentina, New Zealand, and other food producing countries frozen meat or fruits are carried across oceans to feed people half a world away. From there, industrial nations of Europe, North America and east Asia ship out manufactured goods in giant metal boxes – containers – neatly stowed upon container ships.

Our own comfortable way of life depends upon the ships that shift these goods across the expanses of the Earth's oceans and seas.

Navigation aids

Ships could not cross trackless oceans without navigation aids to help crews find their way. Centuries ago, ships' captains had only magnetic compasses to help them keep direction. They worked out the north–south position by using instruments called sextants for measuring the height of the sun or certain stars. And they found their east–west position with the help of accurate clocks called chronometers. Now captains also have help from electronic and other aids. Gyrocompasses show a ship's position with less error than magnetic compasses. Radio signals sent from shore transmitters, and from artificial satellites, help captains plot their position. *Radar* and *sonar* systems warn of nearby rocks or approaching ships. Lighthouses and floating navigation buoys mark paths for ships approaching port.

▲ This lighthouse stands in the sea at Cordouan on the coast of Brittany, northern France. At night ships far away can see the light flashing from the top of the lighthouse tower. Such lights warn ships away from dangerous cliffs or reefs.

EXPLORING THE SEA

We can travel over the dry land on foot, and we can see the Moon through a telescope and map its surface. But the ocean bed is utterly dark and extremely hostile and so very difficult to explore.

The first attempts
Until the present century, the only way to find out about the sea was to lower instruments on long lines, from ships. The sounding lead, with grease or tallow on its base, would tell how deep the water was and bring back a few grains of sand or a few pebbles to show what the bottom was. Thermometers measured the low temperatures below the surface.

After World War 1 'sonar' came into use. Unlike sunlight, sound waves pass easily through water and sonar is used to direct a beam of sound and pick up the echoes reflected back. In this way we can 'see' shoals of fish, or map the finest details of the sea bed. The sonar transmitter is fixed to the hull of a ship or towed on the end of a long rope so that its beam spreads over the bottom. Other instruments, such as thermometers and current-meters, are anchored to the sea bed where they record measurements for some weeks or months before cutting themselves free and rising for collection.

Cameras, too, can be left for some time at the sea bed, occasionally taking flash pictures. In this way they photograph the marine creatures going about their daily lives without disturbing them.

Nowadays more and more oceanography is done from satellites. They carry instruments that can measure the height of waves, the surface temperatures, the sea's coloration and even detect the presence of shoals of fish.

DESCENDING TO THE DEPTHS

However good our oceanographic instruments, people still want to go down to great depths. But the human body is not built to breathe under great pressure or keep warm in cold water. So anyone going down deep needs protection.

▲ This free-swimming diver uses an aqualung – a breathing device developed in France by Jacques-Yves Cousteau. The diver breathes in fresh air stored in the canister on his back. Breathed-out air forms the bubbles you see floating up. The aqualung is a scuba system. (Scuba is short for *s*elf *c*ontained *u*nderwater *b*reathing *a*pparatus.)

Canals and ports
Modern ocean-going ships have other advantages unknown to early mariners. Two are broad, man-made waterways – short cuts across the continents of North America and Africa. The Suez Canal through Egypt shortens the voyage from England to Sri Lanka by 5600km (3500 miles). The Panama Canal through Panama cuts 16,000km (10,000 miles) off the ocean journey from New York to San Francisco.

Lastly, engineers have built great ports to handle ships and help them load and unload cargoes. Piers, harbour walls and other structures line long tracts of coast, creating man-made shores. The Port of New York and New Jersey – the world's largest port – had a natural advantage because of the many inlets and islands.

But travel is only one of the ways in which we use, and change, the sea.

Divers

Several kinds of diving suit help people to descend below the sea. One type has a glass-fronted helmet and heavy boots, weighing the diver down to prevent him floating up off the sea bed. Below the waterproof outer suit the diver might wear as many as four layers of warm underclothes. Air is pumped down to the diver through a hose. Insulated wires heat the woollen undersuit electrically, and other wires carry spoken messages between the diver and the support vessel on the surface.

Such suits are rather cumbersome. Divers can move around more freely if they carry their own air supply and swim instead of walk on the sea bed. Instead of heavy boots these so-called *scuba* divers usually wear broad flippers.

By the 1970s some divers had gone down to depths of 450m (1476ft). But diving to great depths brings problems. Deep down, water presses so hard on your body that only high-pressure air can fill your lungs. But this forces nitrogen gas into your blood. If you rise too fast the gas forms bubbles that can paralyze or kill you. To prevent that, divers must rise slowly; the deeper and longer they dive the more time they must take coming up. Someone who has spent an hour 120m (385ft) below the surface must allow 27 hours for slowly rising to the surface, or resting in a decompression chamber.

Underwater vessels

While divers were still plodding through shallow waters close to coasts, inventors had begun to build containers to take men breathing air at normal pressure deep below the sea. Success came in 1930 when engineers made a heavy steel ball called a bathysphere. A scientist could sit inside and gaze out through its thick windows as a ship lowered the bathysphere into the ocean. In this way the American naturalist William Beebe became the first man to study and photograph deep-sea creatures 900m (3000ft) below the surface.

Then, in 1960, a strange craft called the *Trieste* took two men to the bottom of the deepest ocean trench on Earth. This bathyscaphe withstood pressures great enough to squash an ordinary submarine. Unlike the bathysphere, the bathyscaphe was not tethered to the surface. But it could travel only up or down.

Meanwhile inventors were building small craft designed to dive deeply and travel to and fro. The first submersible built for underwater exploration was the *Soucoupe*, built in 1959 for the French explorer Jacques Cousteau. The *Soucoupe* could go down to a depth of only 300m (1000ft). Some later submersibles have plunged even deeper.

▼ The bathyscaphe *Trieste* sank 10,917m (35,820ft) to the floor of the Pacific Ocean in 1960. Two men sat in the metal sphere slung below the striped float filled with petrol. To rise they dropped a heavy load of iron shot.

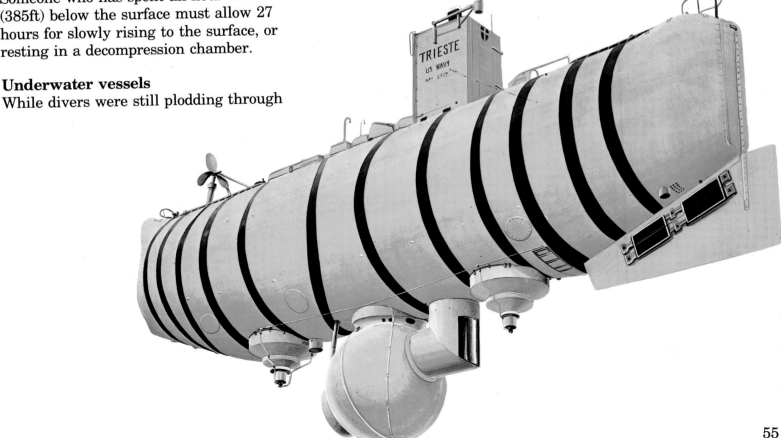

WORKING UNDER WATER

Divers and submersibles can do much more than just explore under water. They can work there, too. There are many kinds of work for them to do. Surveying sites is one. Other tasks are tunnelling, building bridges, and laying cables and pipes. Divers also help to recover sunken ships. They inspect the submerged legs of oil rigs, and clean or mend broken underwater structures.

Underwater work is often difficult. The light is usually dim, the water cold and muddy. Because water robs a diver of his weight, a power drill tends to spin his body around. Also you might think it impossible to paint or burn through metal in the sea. In fact, divers reckon they can tackle all the tasks that people can perform on land.

Divers' tools
Underwater workers have many tools and instruments to help them. Surveyors use power drills to take rock samples. Clamps tether the surveyors to their workplace so that the drills penetrate rock instead of simply whirling men around. Laser rangefinders help surveyors to plot building foundations or routes for pipes. The rangefinders give off green light that travels well through water except where it is cloudy. When working in cloudy water, surveyors use a tape measure, with a compass, to find their bearings.

Other aids help divers to locate and repair underwater damage. For instance, ultrasonic sensors and television cameras might show up rust or cracks in underwater joints. Divers can use blow torches to cut away damaged metal. Epoxy resin patches help them mend holes in certain pipes. And powered rotating saws easily slice through underwater cables tangled around a ship's propeller.

Equally important are the tools that help to protect underwater structures from damage. Divers regularly scrub ships' hulls with powered brushes to remove barnacles and other encrustations. People can even paint pipes under water to protect them from corrosion: the paint flows from a tube with a paintbrush at one end.

Submersible workhorses
Submersibles equipped with robot arms and other aids can often work as well as divers – sometimes better. In the 1960s American submersibles found and brought up an unexploded hydrogen bomb that had fallen into the sea off Spain. The bomb lay 950m (3100ft) deep – too deep for ordinary divers.

Nowadays submersibles regularly help with cable laying and inspection, and with oil- or gas-rigs standing in the shallow seas off Europe, Asia and North America. Some submersibles have crews. Others are controlled by men at the surface. These remotely controlled devices do much of the dull work of checking the condition of underwater structures. Submersibles that swim have now been joined by trench-diggers and bulldozers that crawl or roll along the bottom of the sea.

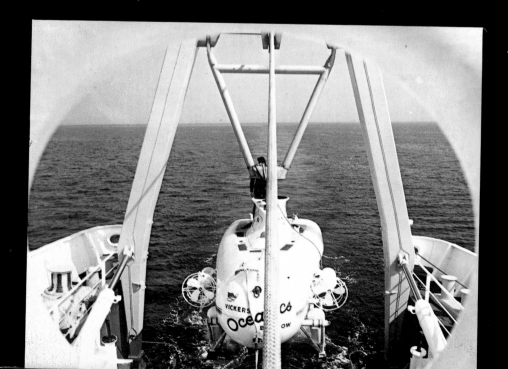

▼ A special ship launches a small submersible designed for working on the sea bed. Such submersibles carry a two-man crew who inspect seabed pipes and use a mechanical arm to gather samples of seabed rock. Twin propellers thrust the vessel through the depths.

▲ This diver is swimming over a wreck, making a preliminary survey to see if it is worth salvaging. If it is, there will be a more detailed survey to work out the best way to salvage as much as possible of the

▶ An underwater archaeologist explores an ancient wreck. Every piece will be recorded in position before it is brought to the surface. In this way ships that sank several thousand years ago have been recorded, recovered and

HARVESTING THE DEEP

Even before people first adventured out in boats the sea would have served them as a valuable larder. Stone Age people plucked tasty shellfish from the rock pools along the shore. Some learnt to fish with lines and nets from the beach. Today, sea fish provide the world with 60 million tonnes of food each year.

Sea fisheries

Most of the world's fishing grounds are over the continental shelves, such as the North Sea and the North Atlantic margins. For here winds and currents stir the waters, providing plenty of food for the fish, so that the harvest is good. Elsewhere any possible supply of food falls from the plankton layer to the deep ocean floor and is lost. Only where cold water surges up bringing these nutrients back to the surface, as off the coast of Peru, is a food supply plentiful enough to support a large number of fish, and with it, the many birds and mammals that feed upon them.

But different fish feed at different depths. Herring, mackerel, sardines and tuna are surface swimming, or pelagic, fishes. Cod, haddock and plaice are

▲ A small inshore cod fishing trawler. The cod caught today are smaller than they used to be because there is so much fishing that the fish do not have a chance to grow large.

◄ A mixed catch of bottom-living fish lies in the hold of this trawler.

▼ Two different methods of catching fish commercially. Shoals of herring and other free-swimming fish are caught by their gills as they try to get through the small mesh holes in the drift net. Nets like these may be several kilometres long. Fish that live on the sea bed, such as flat fish, are caught in conical nets. These are dragged along the sea bed and are kept open by the pressure of the water pushing the otter boards outwards. The fish lying in the hold (**left**) were caught in a net like this.

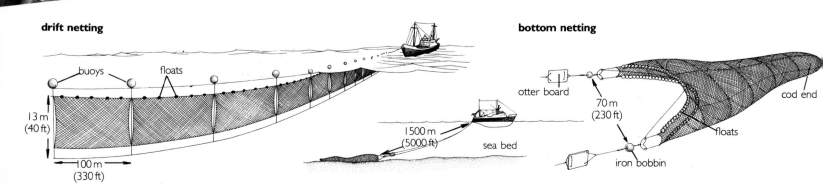

drift netting

buoys   floats

13 m
(40 ft)

100 m
(330 ft)

1500 m
(5000 ft)

sea bed

bottom netting

otter board

70 m
(230 ft)

cod end

floats

iron bobbin

58

demersal fish – that means they are bottom dwellers.

Modern fishing fleets have remarkably efficient ways of finding and catching fish of both these groups. For instance, scientists can tell fishermen exactly where some species feed, and where they breed. Then, too, sonar systems help fishing boats track down shoals. A forward-scan sonar device can even find a shoal at a distance of 4.8km (3 miles).

Trawlers catch bottom-dwelling fishes by hauling trawl nets across the sea bed. Other craft purse (close) a purse seine net around *pelagic* shoals. Drift-netting involves hanging a long net curtain across a stretch of sea.

Long-lining is another fishing method: this time fishes are caught on scores of hooks hanging from long lines paid out across a stretch of sea.

Groups of up to 30 fishing boats supply fish for one big factory ship, where the fish is frozen before being taken back to shore.

Fish is just one kind of food won from the sea. Until whales started growing scarce, they provided such nations as Japan with useful quantities of meat. Shellfish is another useful seafood. Indeed a rich mussel bed can yield more meat than an equal area of meadow grazed by cattle. Then, too, the thrifty Japanese eat large quantities of certain kinds of seaweed. They even grow the plants on nets covering huge tracts of the shallow waters of their Inland Sea.

Mining the sea
Oceans give us more than food. Their waters and the rocks below the sea provide industry with useful chemicals and other substances.

From sea water, special processes extract salt, magnesium iodide and bromine, Magnesium is an ingredient in strong, light, metal alloys; bromine plays a part in medicine, dyeing, photography, and the manufacture of motor fuel and metals.

From shallow seas, dredging vessels suck up gravels, sand and tin; and even off the coast of South Africa, diamonds. From platforms standing in the Gulf of Mexico, North Sea and other shallow waters, engineers pipe gas and oil up to the surface.

Soon, special ships will suck or haul up millions of metallic lumps from the deep floor of the open ocean. Called manganese nodules, the lumps contain not only manganese but cobalt, copper, nickel and other useful substances. As mines on land become exhausted, we shall depend more and more for certain minerals upon new mines beneath the sea.

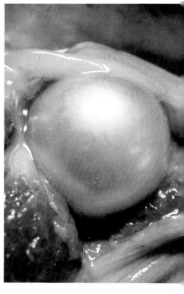

▲ This lovely pearl may end up on a lady's necklace. Oysters manufacture pearls around sand grains or other small irritating substances that find their way inside the oysters' shells.

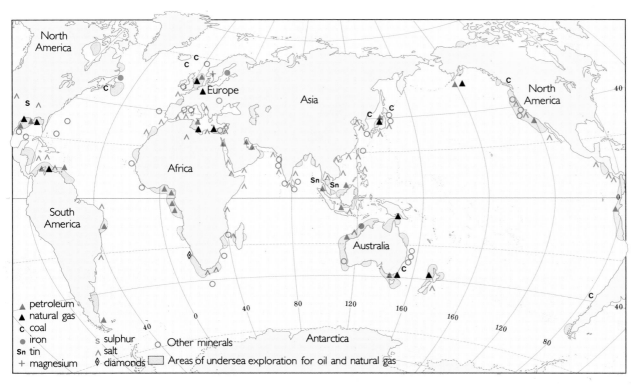

petroleum
natural gas
c coal
iron
Sn tin
+ magnesium
s sulphur
Other minerals
salt
diamonds
Areas of undersea exploration for oil and natural gas

◄ This map shows the world distribution of mineral resources in the oceans. Most of these resources appear to be near land partly because the underlying geology causes them to be there and partly because it is cheaper to exploit resources close to land than in mid-ocean.

SAVING THE SEAS

▲ Conservationists believe that the oceans are in great danger. They are polluted and contaminated by the dumping of nuclear waste (**inset**) and animals such as the whale (**above**) have been hunted so much that they are in danger of becoming extinct.

When this century began, fishermen and whalers thought that oceans would always hold more fish and whales than they could catch. People also thought that cities, factories and ships could pour their wastes into the seas forever without poisoning the waters. This is not true.

Saving whales and fishes
By the 1960s so many whales had been

killed that certain species seemed likely to become extinct. Among these was the blue whale.

By the 1970s overfishing threatened to destroy certain kinds of fish valued as food by humans. North Atlantic catches of cod, haddock, halibut and herring all dwindled.

Luckily most fishing and whaling nations may have acted just in time. They banned the catching of certain species until numbers multiplied. This has saved fish threatened with extinction. But whales breed slowly: by the middle 1980s no one could be sure that all endangered kinds of whale were safe.

Anyway, limiting the catch leaves unsolved this problem: how the sea can help to feed the world's rapidly growing human population. One solution might be to catch and eat more of such plentiful but little eaten animals as kapelin, lantern fish and squids. Another answer might be to eat the shrimp-like krill that many whales and fish feed on.

Cleaning the sea

Catching too many whales and fish is just one way of injuring the seas. Releasing wastes into the sea causes even more extensive damage. Sewage and chemical wastes have poisoned some shallow seas and killed many of their plants and animals. In parts of the Baltic, Black, Caribbean and Mediterranean seas, fish and shellfish have died off in their millions.

Much of the trouble comes from pipes that pour untreated sewage from cities into shallow coastal waters. As it decays sewage consumes oxygen, thus indirectly suffocating fish. Germs that breed in sewage poison shellfish and make bathing dangerous. Beaches also suffer when supertankers sink and spill huge quantities of oil. This clogs seabirds' feathers and coats the shore in sticky 'tar'.

Refineries and factories cause trouble, too, when they let heavy metals such as mercury escape into the sea. In the 1960s, mercury paralyzed many of the Japanese who had eaten shellfish contaminated by this poison.

Yet other poisons enter seas with pesticides washed off farmlands into rivers. Some pesticides accumulate in the livers of fish until the fish are dangerous to eat.

Until recently, most scientists thought it safe to seal some deadly poisons in containers and drop these into deep ocean trenches. But studies show that the poisons could leak out and drift with ocean currents right around the world.

Luckily, many governments are waking up to these dangers. At least some have passed laws to help clean up the seas. Many nations have agreed to stop releasing deadly substances into the sea. Already dangerous pesticides are disappearing from northern oceans. Also, oil companies have invented new ways of tackling oil spilt at sea: they can even use bacteria to eat up some oil as food.

Also a few nations have set aside marine parks, so that coral reefs or other offshore areas of special beauty are never tampered with.

Now, marine biologists around the world keep watch on the purity of seas. Unfortunately keeping offshore waters clean costs money that poor countries can ill afford; the oceans will stay healthy and productive only if nations can and will take notice of the 'watchdogs'' warnings.

◄ Coral reefs bathed by transparent seas die back where pollution poisons offshore waters in the tropics. In places, coral is even quarried for building stone or gravel. But at last some governments have started to protect these underwater worlds.

GLOSSARY

Abyss The deepest part of the ocean.
Atoll A low ring of limy rock enclosing a lagoon, an area of salt water.
Ball and socket joint Type of joint where the rounded end of a bone or other similar structure fits into a cup-shaped socket. This type of joint allows a great range of movement. There is a ball and socket joint where your arm meets your shoulder.
Bar Long, low beach lying just offshore.
Bivalve Sea creature such as an oyster or clam with two shells.
Cay Low island formed where sea has piled up enough sand so that it shows above the surface.
Chlorophyll The food-producing substance found only in green plants.
Coelenterate Animal, such as a jellyfish or sea anemone, that has a pouch-shaped gut in which it digests its food.
Continental shelf The underwater rock platform that surrounds continents.
Coriolis effect The term used to describe the way the Earth's spin steers currents to the right north of the equator and to the left south of the equator.
Crustaceans Animals such as crabs and lobsters with a hard, crust-like shell.

Delta New land formed in the sea at the mouths of large rivers. The land is built up from the mud and silt brought down by the river.
Drift A deep sea current.
Dune Sand hills formed where wind-blown sand has been deposited against an obstacle.
Ebbing Term used to describe a tide that is going out.
Echinoderm Sea creature with skin that is usually spiny. The group includes starfish and sea urchins.
Estuary The mouth of a river.
Evaporate To lose moisture. The moisture does not disappear, it turns into vapour. The vapour will form clouds and, eventually, rain.
Floe Huge slab of floating ice.
Flowing Term used to describe a tide that is coming in.
Frazil ice The first thin film of ice that forms over sea water.
Gills The organs with which fish and other animals that live under water breathe.
Glacier Slowly moving river-like mass of immensely thick ice.
Gravity The force of attraction exerted by all bodies in the universe.

▼ European lobsters caught in a pot. If the lobsters are below a certain size they have to be put back in the sea, otherwise they would soon become extinct.

▼ Animals, such as crabs and lobsters, which have hard shells must shed the shells from time to time if they are to grow. This Pacific lobster has just shed its old shell which is lying on the rock.

Groyne Long man-made barrier running from the land out into the sea to prevent the sea washing away a beach.

Gyres The great loops in which the ocean currents flow.

Iceberg Floating mass of ice that has broken off a glacier where it has slid into the sea.

Key See cay.

Lagoon Shallow stretch of sea water almost cut off from the sea by a low sandbank.

Larva (plural **larvae**) The young of animals like crabs. Often they do not look like the adults at all. (Like insects, they go through a larval stage before developing into adults.)

Longshore drift The way that waves and tides can make sand or pebbles zig-zag along the coast until they are finally thrown up on a beach.

Mantle The layer of hot rock below the Earth's surface.

Medusa (plural **medusae**) One of the stages a young jellyfish goes through before it develops into an adult.

Molluscs Soft-bodied animals, usually with hard protective shells; for example, limpets and snails.

Molten Another way of saying melted, although molten is usually used to describe something that does not melt easily.

Pack ice A great field of ice formed from many floes packed tightly together.

Pelagic The upper layers of the open ocean.

Phosphorescence The radiant glow given off at night by some types of plankton.

Phytoplankton Planktonic plants.

Plankton Minute plants and animals that live in large numbers in the oceans.

Polyp Individual member of a large colony of, for example, coral.

Radar System using short radio waves to find out the direction and speed and distance of objects. The word comes from Radio Detection And Ranging.

Salinity The amount of salt in something.

Scuba Self-Contained Underwater Breathing Apparatus used by divers.

Sedentary Remaining in one place either for long periods or all the time.

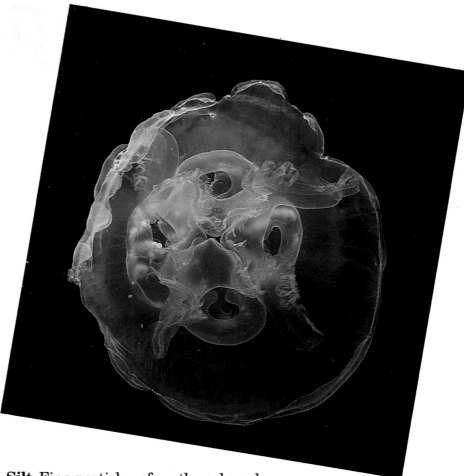

Silt Fine particles of earth and mud carried by rivers. It is often deposited at the river's mouth where the river's speed becomes so slow that the silt particles sink to the bottom.

Sonar System for detecting underwater objects with reflected sound. The word comes from SOund NAvigation and Ranging.

Spit A beach that grows out into the sea from a headland.

Stipe The central 'stem' of a piece of seaweed.

Tsunamis Vast waves caused by underwater earthquakes or volcanoes.

Zooplankton Planktonic animals.

▲ The common jellyfish reaches about 25cm (10in) in diameter. Its transparent body, here photographed from below, has a slightly blue tinge.

◄ An elephant seal lies flat on a beach. Such earless seals are not able to lift themselves off the ground as well as eared seals can. Elephant seals get their name from the large, drooping noses of the males.

INDEX

Acknowledgements
Heather Angel; Ardea; Camera Press; John Clegg; Bruce Coleman; Daily Telegraph Colour Library; Peter David; Martin Dohrn; Greenpeace; Brian Hawkes; Archivio IGDA/Archivio B, C Annunziata, C Bevilacqua, Cedri, N Cirani, G Giacomelli, C Gualco, Maltini-Solaini A Margiocco, G Mazza, P2; Jacana; NHPA; National Film Board of Canada; Naval Photographic Center USA; Picturepoint; Popperfoto; Science Photo Library; Spectrum Colour Library; Vickers Ltd.